Video Marketing for Entrepreneurs

From Selfie to Network TV + Bonus Tips

Red Carpet
ACADEMY

Author
Anita Miranda

Co-Author
Samantha Leiter

Video Marketing for Entrepreneurs
From Selfie to Network TV + Bonus Tips

Living Disabled Publishing
Publication Date: 2016
First Edition, 2016
©2016 Miranda's Creatives, LLC. All Rights Reserved
Printed in USA
1098765 4321

Color Edition ISBN: 978-0692609378
Black and White Edition ISBN: 978-0692609392
Workbook Color Edition ISBN: 978-0692611920
Workbook Black and White Edition ISBN: 978-0692610060

Author: Anita Miranda
Co-author: Samantha Leiter
Edited & Illustrated by: Samantha Leiter
Design, Layout, and Graphics Design: Samantha Leiter & Anita Miranda
Cover Design: Barb Anderson

Contact the Author:
Anita Miranda:
transform@anitamiranda.com
www.AnitaMiranda.com

~Dedication~

To other entrepreneurs who have the courage to start their own business and to fearless leaders in their industry who want to be "Pitch Perfect."

~Acknowledgments~

Anita Miranda with Circle of Helping Hands, a 501(c)(3) (COHH) is grateful for the contributors and the participants of the very first Red Carpet Academy Workshop held in San Diego, CA. Also to Felena Hanson and her staff who offered her amazing Hera Hub co-working space to set our stage.

Proceeds from Red Carpet Academy media kit benefits COHH's mission, to assist Veterans, Women and their Children by providing Advocacy, Career Skills and Community Involvement.

Keynote Speakers:

Felena Hanson
Jenn Kaye
Angela Chee
Natalia Robert

Bonus Tips Contributors:

Holly Kolman
Barb Anderson
Anne McColl
Giselle Fox
Skyler McCurine, copywriting

Participants:

Laurie Itkin
Gail Kraft
Holly Kolman
Kaliani Cynthia Hupper
Skyler McCurine
Jenny D. Beato
Karen D. L. Kramer
Susan Atooli
Anne-Marie Diggle Rabago
Elena-Lene Gravgaard
Ellen Scott Grable

Media PRO and More Staff Volunteers:

Samantha Leiter
Carrie Brooks
Mathew Hupper
Mike from Chicago (our homeless man who I never got his last name)

~Keynote Speakers~

Jenn Kaye - Head-On Communications & Touch With Intention

Jenn is an internationally recognized communication and lifestyle expert, author and media personality. Principal of Head-On Communications LLC, she is known for helping her clients and audiences align their businesses, brand and lifestyle with their unique and authentic expression.

With a background in languages (Japanese, Spanish, French & a little Russian), wellness, entertainment and personal transformation, Jenn has a special way of translating your message into an experience that not only creates greater connection with your market and audience, it reminds you of your own magnificence and contribution in the world.

Having facilitated a diversity of world class groups for over 20 years, such as the U.S. Government's Department of Defense; including the Marines, Air Force, and Army; Capital One, The Atlantis Hotel, Royal Caribbean Cruise Lines and Kaiser Permanente Health Systems, she continues tp passionately coach and consult with leaders who are ready to live their life head-on and are committed to making a difference.

Felena Hanson - Hera Hub

Felena is a long-time entrepreneur and marketing maven. Her 20 year career has spanned from technology start-ups to digital marketing agencies. Some of her former clients include DirecTV, Epson, CNN, and Union Bank. Before becoming an entrepreneur she was Director of Marketing for a venture-backed San Diego internet company that sold to America Online in 2003.

As Felena launched her first business, Perspective Marketing, she found her passion for supporting other female entrepreneurs through leadership roles with several professional women's organizations, including Ladies Who Launch and Women's Global Network.

Her latest venture, Hera Hub, is a spa-inspired shared workspace and community for female entrepreneurs. This as-needed, flexible work and meeting space provides a productive environment for growing businesses. Hera Hub members have access to a professional space to meet with clients and to connect and collaborate with like-minded business owners, thus giving them the support they need to be prosperous. The business supports hundreds of freelancers, entrepreneurs, and nonprofits in over 16 industry segments.

After building three successful locations, she franchised the business and is expanding across the United States. Her next goal is to support over 20,000 women in the launch and growth of their business by 2020.

Felena is passionate about education, earning her Bachelor's degree in Marketing from the University of San Diego and her MBA from California State University Dominguez Hills. She taught Marketing and Entrepreneurship at the Fashion Institute of Design & Merchandising and at California State University Dominguez Hills for the MBA online program for eight years.

Felena and Hera Hub have been featured in Inc Magazine, the BBC News, Forbes, and the New York Times. She has been nominated for numerous small business awards and has been rewarded for her efforts by winning the 2012 "Women Business Owner of the Year" award and the 2014 "Women Advocate of the Year" award from the San Diego chapter of the National Organization of Women Business Owners. In 2014 she also won the "Small Business Champion of the Year" award from the San Diego Small Business Administration.

Natalia Robert - Full Circle Images

Natalia has been photographing life for over 15 years and is bringing her unique eye to spaces and businesses all over Southern California. Her world travels, love of the outdoors, and fun energy blend perfectly for a memorable photo session that is tailor-made to each client. Her years in architecture and graphic arts, meanwhile, bring a keen design eye to all final images. While Natalia is always happy behind a camera, she especially enjoys photographing beautiful homes, as well as collaborating with fellow local business owners to refine their branding images.

Angela Chee - Zen Media Inc.

Angela Chee is a Host, Writer, Speaker and Founder of Zen Media Inc., a media training and consulting company. She helps companies and individuals grow their business and brand by more effectively sharing their product, service and message with the media. With more than 15 years of experience in the broadcast industry, Angela is an award-winning journalist who has worked as an Anchor/Reporter for KNBC-TV and KCBS/KCAL-TV in Los Angeles, Fox 6 in San Diego, E! Entertainment Television, and hosted shows for HGTV (Home and Garden Television), The International Channel, Channel One News and helped launch Entertainment Tonight China. Merging her traditional media background with her social media influence she is also the Founder of The Zen Mom.com, an informative and inspirational website with the mission to empower through wisdom, inspiration and laughter and The Zen Mom TV. She has also been a contributor for various sites including Lifetime Moms, Momversation, Patch, and Mom Logic.

Anita Miranda - Miranda's Creatives, LLC & Circle of Helping Hands

Anita Miranda is a media and self-help entrepreneur with several years of experience helping women and men become prepared for on-camera appearances and showing them how to look and act their best while the camera is pointed at them. She recently developed Red Carpet Academy for those who are preparing to be in front of, or want to be behind the camera, shooting their own videos in the convenience of their own home or office. She also penned her autobiography: *Anita Miranda, PTSD and Me: How Bill Clinton Got Me Out of Bed.*

She is the co-founder and Creative Director of Mirandas Creatives, LLC, a company that prepares leaders on how to present themselves in the best possible light when they are on camera, mostly geared towards corporate and business professionals who need to give interviews, present materials, or have to be filmed for other reasons. Every client receives the VIP experience.

Anita Miranda has a Master's Degree in Education and a Bachelor's Degree in Business Administration with decades of experience in the field. She is also the founder and current president of the Circle of Helping Hands, a nonprofit advocacy group and skill set training center. She is a retired, disabled veteran of the Navy. Anita lives in Scottsdale, AZ.

~ Foreword ~

It's a new day; it's a new quarter and it's going to be the best one yet, I can feel it. Public speaking is known to be one of our greatest "fears." Now, let's add a couple of photographers, videographers and a live microphone? This would rank pretty high in our fear factor wouldn't you agree? I know how it feels to be in front and behind the camera. And both are not easy feats. I am not a celebrity or a spokes model nor a natural beauty. I wanted to create a production set to help women be seen, be heard and be beautiful. What we at Red Carpet Academy provide are the tools, experience and practicum to be camera ready.

Red Carpet Academy is your first step to preparing for your camera ready, anytime anywhere opportunities. This DIY media kit is a smart investment for you and your company's future. You will feel confident in front of the camera, behind the camera, and implement Red Carpet strategies to grow your company along with new friends and colleagues to help you achieve it.

We have assembled a great line-up of industry experts, ready to share their practical tools, relevant topics and useful strategies for your video needs. Expect to be amazed and entertained while energizing your mind, maximizing your skills and empowering you to feel and look beautiful no matter what shape and size.

Thank you so much for entrusting us with your most precious commodity: You!

Truly Honored,

Anita Miranda and Team

Table of Contents

~ In Front of The Camera ~

Techniques and Tips For Appearing on Video

RedCarpetAcademy.org

When it comes to being on camera, not all people are naturals, surprise, surprise. This is why there are such a select number of people that are actually hired to work behind and on video. There are numerous natural slip-ups that people make, thinking they are a full-fledged natural.

The Ben Stein Effect: These people shut their personality off the second the camera starts to roll. It can be nerves or their sheer lack of interest, regardless it doesn't work.

The Silver Tongue: I love to talk, a lot. However, there is such a thing as over communicating. You shouldn't need hours upon hours to explain yourself; your mission or your product.

The Grinch: You should be honored to share your message on camera. Someone found you interesting enough to listen to. So be thankful, turn that frown upside down. Even the Grinch received a heart.

Dr. Know-it-all: We get it. You're a subject matter expert. You received 18 PhDs and one of them was honorary from the Dalai Lama himself. This may be so but sharing your intelligence in a self-indulgent tone lacks wisdom.

The "Winging-It": You're laid back. You like to go with the flow; you wear Piccuhuli and enjoy linen pants. Your motto is "no stress" and whatever shall be, will be. Do not take this approach towards the camera. You must be prepared. Video and a crew can be expensive. Respect everyone's time and your pocketbook by being prepared, mindful, and organized. Know your content.

This book was designed for **YOU**, yes wonderful you, especially if you fall into one or more of the categories above. Have no fear my friend; you will be camera ready by the time this book is through with you!

4

~Speaking~

6

How Do You Speak?

At home, record your voice. Listen to how you articulate.

Are you breathy? Do you pause for too long?

Do you speak too quickly? Etc. People are often surprised to

hear how they sound after the video is complete.

Even the greatest singers in history did sound checks to ensure that they were audible.
If Aretha Franklin can do it, you can too.

LIGHTS, CAMERA ACTION

Write How You Speak

When writing a script for a teleprompter, write it how you would actually speak it. It is easier just to read it straight from the teleprompter than trying to paraphrase what you are reading.

Hello, I'm here

Do you remember having to read out-loud in school? Remember stumbling over the words as you tried to read them and speak them at the same time? You'll get much the same problem trying to read something from the teleprompter. Writing your script the way you naturally speak, however, helps with this problem.

LIGHTS, CAMERA ACTION

Notecards

It is always a good idea to practice several times before going on camera. Try using notecards to jot down your main points and practice saying them, but not word for word. This can help by giving you structure without having to memorize every little thing.

When Oprah Winfrey first started in the broadcast industry, she placed notecards on her lap and discreetly took a peek once in a while. One day, a reporter asked her what her notecards said. She answered, 'Nothing, I noticed that Barbara Walters always had notecards, so I do too." If you have Oprah's DNA for memorization, then you may skip your notecards.

LIGHTS, CAMERA ACTION

Full Sentences

When you are being interviewed, repeat the questions and answer in complete sentences. Also, do not refer to previous statements, for example "Like I previously stated."

> Like I previously stated. Stories with depth and emotion.

VS

> We want stories with depth and emotion.

Speak complete. Sentences. Not easy to follow, right? That's why we speak in complete sentences.

LIGHTS. CAMERA
ACTION

Countdown

In the news, reporters often countdown "3...2...1..." and then pause before speaking. This gives editors a clean place to start editing and also helps you mentally prepare yourself.

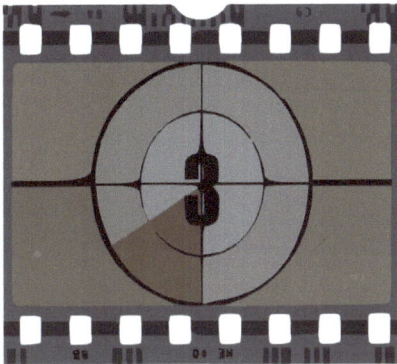

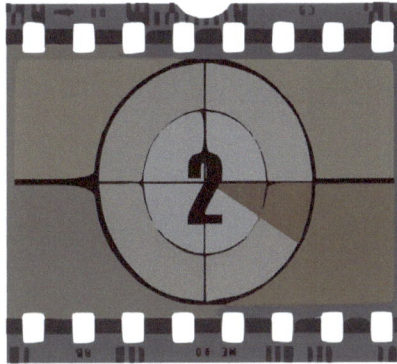

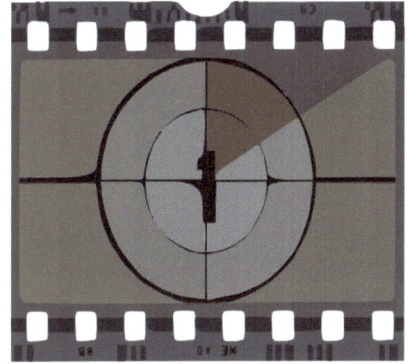

Pause before you speak. If you fudge a take, it will be easier to fix. Also, if you are using multiple pieces of equipment to record audio, use a clapper to make the audio easier to sync in post.

LIGHTS, CAMERA
ACTION

Practice Your Timing

Practice your script and time. A general rule is a 1/3 page runs about 45 seconds. Stay within your time allocated or the editor will have to cut somewhere and it may be your money shot.

"I don't know if I practiced more than anybody, but I sure practiced enough. I still wonder if somebody - somewhere - was practicing more than me."

-Larry Bird

LIGHTS, CAMERA
ACTION

High Vs Low

Try speaking with a lower voice. Lower voices come across as more authoratative and believable; it is often more aesthetically pleasing as well.

Who sounds smoother and more relaxed? Cyndi Lauper or Barry White? The smooth operator and King of Conception himself, Mr. Barry White. I'm not encouraging you to speak in baritone if you're a soprano, but taking your tone an octave deeper can help your message come across authentically and calmly.

LIGHTS, CAMERA ACTION

Keep Your Language Simple

Avoid using special terminology that is specific to your business or

define the terms in a simple and clear manner

so that your audience can easily follow you.

Never use a C47 to hold up a stinger.

VS

Never use a clothespin to hold up an extension cord.

Dr. Subject Matter Expert, we understand that your niche dissertation dissects the root of mitochondrial DNA in aurelius plathenum...What??? Speak in layman terms; this might be your audience's first introduction to your topic, business, idea, etc. So be sure to use words that are at a level that will enable your audience to grasp this new concept.

14

LIGHTS, CAMERA ACTION

Speak At A Steady Pace

Don't speak too fast. You want to speak slowly and concisely so that your audience can understand your message.

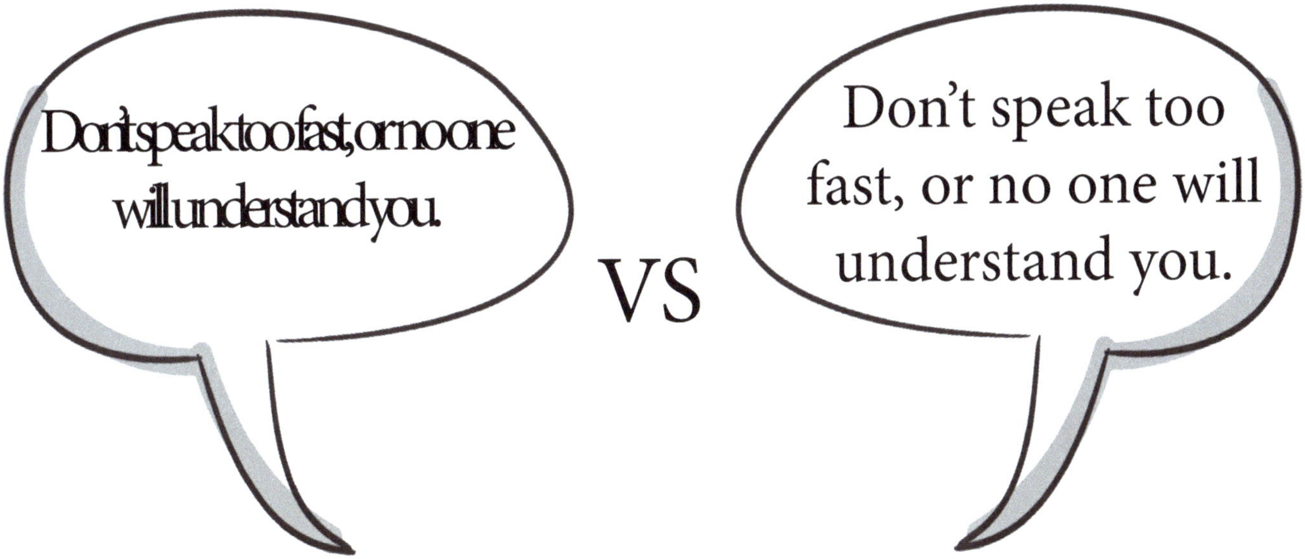

Don't speak too fast, or no one will understand you.

VS

Don't speak too fast, or no one will understand you.

This is not an auction, in which the goal is to say as much as humanly possible with one breathe. Take your time, and make sure you pause where it feels natural. Speak at a normal pace, and your work will sell itself.

RedCarpetAcademy.org

LIGHTS, CAMERA
ACTION

Avoid Monotone

When speaking avoid using a mellow voice, as it can come off as monotone. Try varying your pitch and speed to sound more engaging.

The only time monotone works is with Ben Stein, and he has somehow found a way to make millions from his robotic pitch. Be sure to use volume, range, and variation when you're speaking. This will keep your viewer engaged, and they will hang onto your every word.

LIGHTS, CAMERA
ACTION

Breathe

When you are nervous, you tend to take quick, shallow breathes

or you hold your breathe. Instead, take slow and deep breathes

to help compose yourself.

Whenever I am forced to do sit-ups (because it isn't anything I would ever elect to do), I find myself holding my breath, as if oxygen would keep me from actually sitting up. I intentionally have to tell myself to breathe and allow oxygen to enter my melon head, so that I can lift it off the ground in the hopes of attaining a six-pack. The oxygen actually helps me complete the task, imagine that! Now, be sure to breathe, it will help you as it did me.

LIGHTS, CAMERA
ACTION

Speak From The Abdomen

Don't speak from your chest or throat. Coming from your abdomen adds an extra "oomph" behind your voice.

"If you have what you want to say inside, and if you are crying for something that is true inside, it doesn't matter. The camera always sees it."

-Elena Anaya

~Audio Techniques~

LIGHTS, CAMERA ACTION

"Uhs" and "Ums"

Avoid using the words "uh" and "um."

They make you sound unprofessional and nervous.

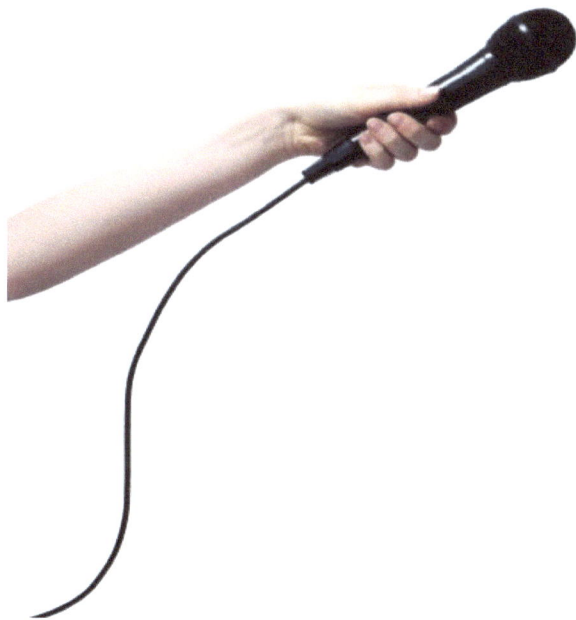

Filler words are plaguing our culture's vernacular. "Uh," "Ah," "Um," "Like," "So..." **STOP**. It's better to breathe and think about your next word than to try and kill time with filler. Google *'Carrie Prejean'* and you will understand the severity of this audible fatal condition.

**LIGHTS, CAMERA
ACTION**

Hide Wires

When using equipment like lavalier microphones,

hide the wires so that they cannot be seen by the camera.

"Every time you get on a stage or in front of a camera, the whole exercise is about imagination. You're constantly depicting something that doesn't exist, and trying to find the reality of it. Once you settle on that premise, everything else is a matter of degrees."

-Ron Perlman

LIGHTS, CAMERA ACTION

Face The Camera

When you have a subject speaking, they need to face forward, towards the camera. Do not film them from the back or from profile.

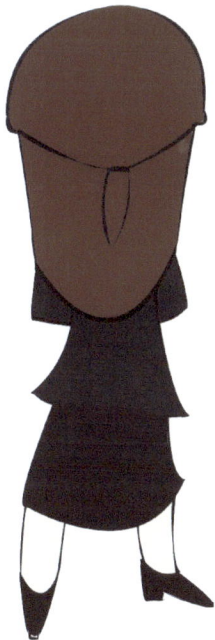

"I am the same on camera as I am off. I can't imagine being any other way."
-Olivia Munn

23

LIGHTS, CAMERA ACTION

Location Audio

When you are filming on location, scout out the area beforehand.

Find a place that is fairly quiet so that the background noise

isn't picked up by the mics.

Like real estate, it is all about the location. Audio is a very particular aspect to your videos. Audio cannot be fixed with background noise. So unless you are designing a music video with lots going on, choose your location wisely.

~ What To Do With ~
Your Hands

Forward Hand Motion

Don't allow your hands to go further than your shoulders.

Emphasize with forward motions, not sideways motion.

"With dancing, you have to know spatial movement with somebody. It is steps. It's literally steps and knowing how close to be or how far away. You have to have the beat in the right place with the camera."

-Channing Tatum

Hands

Keep your hands in front of your body, somewhere between

your chest and your hips. Moving your hands while you speak

is fine, as it adds to your performance.

Here' a golden rule: actions speak louder than words. Listen to your momma and do as she says. Gesturing adds flare and flavor to what could otherwise be drab audio/video. Speak with passionate non-verbal's (minus the middle finger). And be absolutely sure that your gestures are within the frame. Do a test shot.

LIGHTS, CAMERA
ACTION

Movement

When you are speaking in front of the camera, avoid

moving around much. It can seem unprofessional.

Another reason to avoid moving much, especially quickly, is that it can create motion blur. So don't move around too much, unless you *want* to look like the Flash.

~Green Screen~

Green Screen Lighting

Be sure that your green screen is lit evenly and that there are no shadows on the screen. This makes it easier to remove later in post.

Green screen preparation is not easy. However, if you want to try, light the back screen with two lights evenly, and you need to use a separate light for your subject. Preferably two. Make sure you have editing software to "Chroma-key" out the green screen, or all you will have is a beautifully lit green screen. If you want a romantic scene or a space scene, then green screen is definitely for you. However, don't say I didn't warn you.

LIGHTS, CAMERA ACTION

Green Screen Outfits

When filming on a green screen, avoid wearing green clothes,

clothing that is transparant, or anything reflective.

Unless you are preparing to be Jim Carrey in the *Mask*, don't wear green, ever. Do your homework and learn what colors are in the "green" family. Even if that shade of green makes your eyes emerald green, you do not want to be the "invisible" lady or gentleman.

~Lighting~

Avoid Backlighting

Do not light your subject mainly from behind. This often

results in an overly bright "halo" around your subject

and makes their face too dark to properly distinguish their features.

Thou art holy, and the beam of light will draw the audience into humble submission and devout prayer... NOT! Avoid having a white halo surround you. No backlighting.

LIGHTS, CAMERA ACTION

Light Your Subject

Do your best to get your subject properly lit on set.

Video that is too dark or too bright look poor and amateurish.

It is also hard to fix in post.

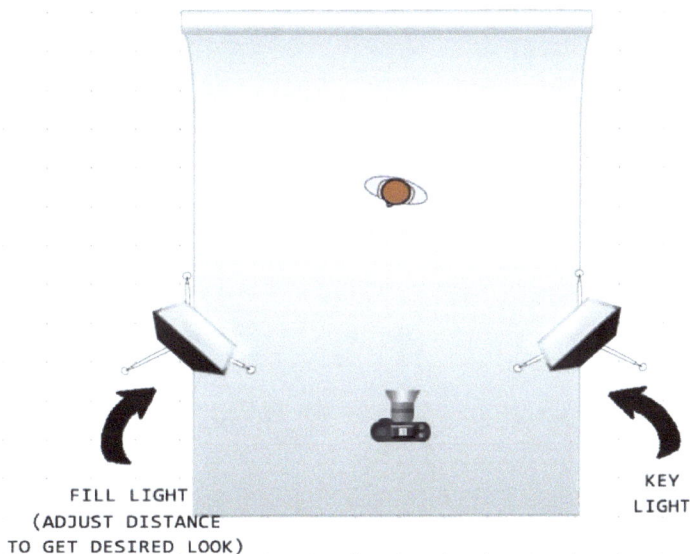

FILL LIGHT
(ADJUST DISTANCE
TO GET DESIRED LOOK)

KEY
LIGHT

You don't want your interviewee to resemble an x-ray or ghost. Do everything in moderation (or so my personal trainer tells me), so avoid minimal and excessive lighting.

~Backgrounds~

40

LIGHTS, CAMERA ACTION

Clean Backgrounds

Avoid having a busy or cluttered background.

It will draw your audience towards the background

and away from your message.

Have you ever seen an episode of *Hoarders*? Notice how they only interview the hoarders in front of a plain background, versus their cluttered house? It's because the audience would be eyeballing everything in the room, as opposed to listening to the program participant's story. Keep your filming room clean, just like momma taught you.

41

~Organization~

44

LIGHTS. CAMERA ACTION

Do Your Research

Video is not the cheapest or quickest method to get your message across, but it is very memorable. To save money and time, do research to see what others have done and figure out what you could do better.

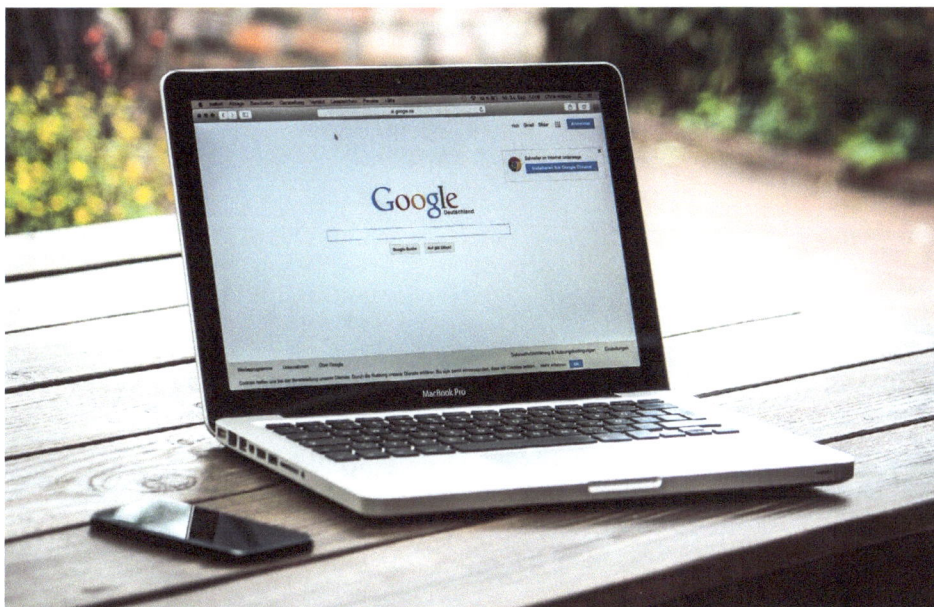

Like a job interview, researching is key. Your brand, your message reflects who you are, what services you provide and if your target audience needs your product. Give the same tenacity as you would for a coveted job position; go the extra mile to earn your customers.

LIGHTS, CAMERA ACTION

Have A Plan

Be sure to plan out your shoot. Have a basic schedule to

know what order everything is going to be shot in.

Today's Schedule

9:00 AM Meet at the office	12:15 PM Break for Lunch
10:00 AM Have equipment set & tests done Practice Scenes	1:00 PM Shoot Scene 3
10:30 AM Shoot Scene 1	2:30 PM Any Extra Shots
11:15 AM Shoot Scene 2	3:30 PM Break Down

Keep an outline handy to help you keep track of the day. No one wants to be part of a hot mess, so keep your shoot orderly and scheduled.

LIGHTS, CAMERA ACTION

Always Have A Plan B

Remember Murphy's Law: "Anything that can go wrong,

will go wrong." Have a back-up plan in case things go wrong.

"Where I think the most work needs to be done is behind the camera, not in front of it."

-Denzel Washington

RedCarpetAcademy.org

LIGHTS, CAMERA ACTION

Keep A Checklist

Keep a checklist of all the equipment you need and check

the list when you pack up so that nothing is left behind.

 Lapel Mic

 Camera

 Scripts

"Be prepared, work hard, and hope for a little luck. Recognize that the harder you work and the better prepared you are, the more luck you might have."

-Ed Bradley

LIGHTS, CAMERA ACTION

Color Coordinating

Buy different colored electrical tape and use them to mark which cords and accessories go with each piece of equipment. This makes it easier to assemble what you need when you are in a hurry.

If you don't know what cord goes to what, you'll waste time. And if you waste time, you mess up your schedule. And messing up your schedule can mess up your plan. So to avoid having a hot mess, use colored electrical tape to match cords with their equipment.

RedCarpetAcademy.org

LIGHTS, CAMERA ACTION

Pack Ahead Of Time

If you need to go to an event, have all of your equipment

sorted and packed the day before.

Imagine your vacation week starts tomorrow and you are going on a cruise. Would you just show up with your passport, ticket, and you? Of course not. Always plan and pack ahead.

LIGHTS, CAMERA ACTION

Create A Storyboard

A storyboard can help you organize your shoot

and see what kind of shots you need to get.

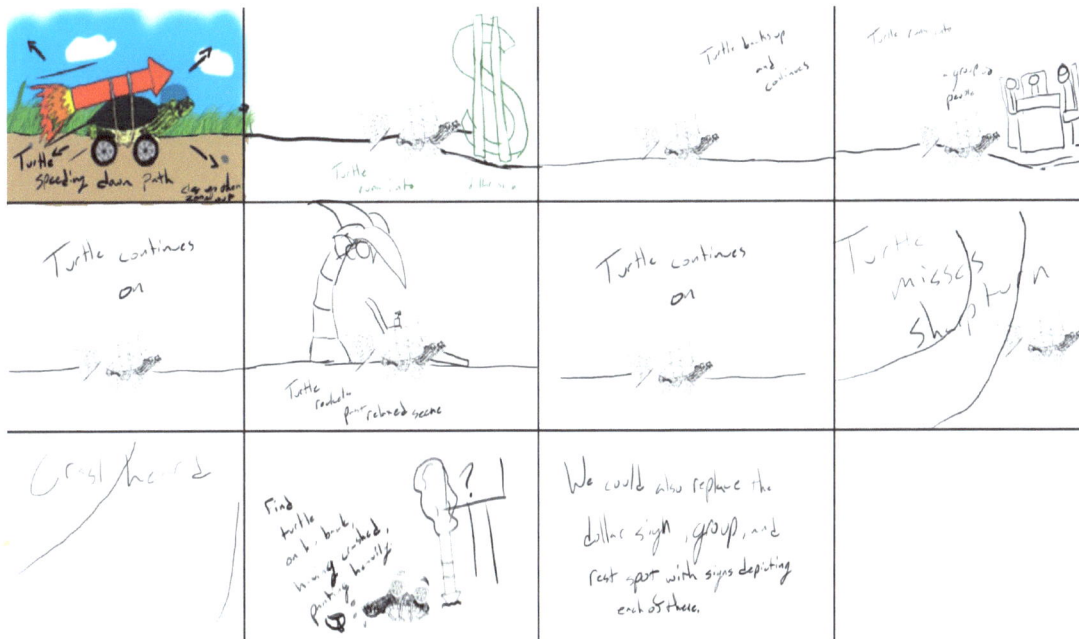

A storyboard will help you keep your shoot in order. It can be challenging to try and remember every detail that you "intended" to shoot.

Sample Storyboard

Intro
_____

_____

_____

_____

_____

_____

_____

_____

_____

_____

Outro
_____

_____

~Behind The Camera~

Techniques and Tips For Working Behind the Scenes

RedCarpetAcademy.org

*C*ongratulations. You want to produce your own videos. But what really goes into a professional video production?

Some people come into video production thinking it won't cost very much and that it takes just a few hours to do. Sometimes it can be that way, but most of the time it isn't. Some of the factors that can determine the cost for digital video productions are:

Experience/Creativity
Equipment
Cost
Time

EXPERIENCE/CREATIVITY

Experience counts for a lot when choosing a producer/videographer/editor. They understand how to spend the time wisely and efficiently. The less experience someone has, the more likely mistakes will show up when you start a production. You can learn how to properly shoot a video. However, creativity comes from the heart.

EQUIPMENT

Equipment is the next consideration. The type used can add a lot of quality and/or cost to a production. Do you want the video production done in HD or SD? HD is going to cost more but that is where all production is going. Most companies have invested $15,000 for a camera, lights, and audio gear. Other invested $30,000 to $100,000 or more. Get the camera that fits your needs.

COST

Preparation and having a successful Creative Session makes a huge difference. This is a very important point: make most of your decisions during pre-production, as making changes mid-production can be very costly. The decision-making process is the most expensive part of any video production and eats up the most time. Which is why the more time you spend on pre-production, the less time is spent making last minute decisions during the actual production, therefore saving you money.

TIME

You can take all of the above-mentioned factors into consideration to help you determine how much time it would take to create your video. The more involved it is the more time it will take. The simpler it is the less time it will take. One is not necessarily better than the other. However, how that time is spent is important.

Necessary
~ Equipment ~

58

LIGHTS. CAMERA ACTION

External Microphones

It is best to use an external microphone instead of the one on your camera. The audio will be clearer.

Did you ever play microphone or rock star when you were little? Now is the time to put that into practice. Make sure to keep the microphone near your lips. If possible, lay the side of the microphone's windscreen on your chin.

Audio Levels

When checking the audio, always speak at the same level

that you will use when the camera is rolling.

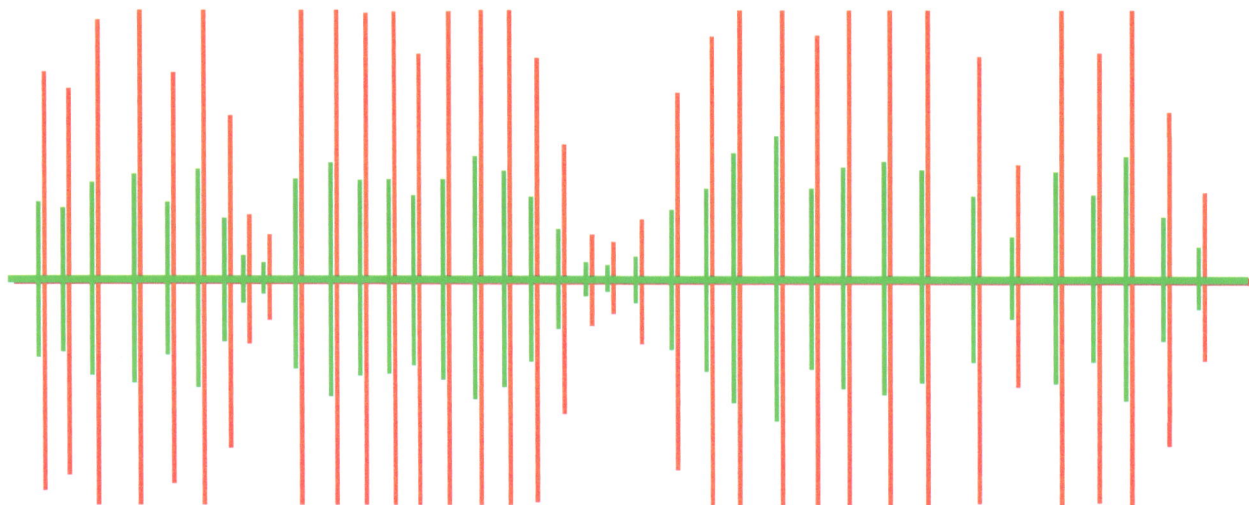

My grandfather was a very mellow and even-keeled man. He never shouted...except when he was on the telephone. We used to laugh hysterically when this soft-tempered man would pick up the phone and start yelling into the receiver. It's as though he believed he was speaking to someone with little to no hearing on the other end, all the time. Some people go ballistic the second the record button starts. There is no need to scream on camera; you will be heard. It's important to do an audio test before filming, so you know how loud and soft you can/should speak.

60

LIGHTS, CAMERA ACTION

Lapel Mics

Be careful where you place a lapel microphone.

Hair and jewelry will wreak havoc on your audio.

"Everywhere you go you hear things that are untrue. You've just got to learn that if I don't say it, physically out of my mouth, on camera, it's not true."
-Selena Gomez

RedCarpetAcademy.org

Use Fast Cards

When filming with a camera that requires SD cards, you want

ones that work fast and have alot of space. You should use

cards that are 300x or faster and are at least 8GB.

16 GB

"The camera makes everyone a tourist in other people's reality, and eventually in one's own."
-Susan Sontag

LIGHTS, CAMERA ACTION

Keep A Spare On Hand

It is always a good idea to have extras of everything,

from batteries to lights.

A woman has an average of 40 items in her purse. Carrying extra items for a rainy day isn't just a female thing either; George Castanza stuffed his wallet with decade old receipts and Joey carried a man bag (a.k.a. a satchel) on *Friends*. Bags, purses, and pouches: Use them. Pack extra equipment, makeup, and resources with you, especially if you are shooting remotely and won't be able to make a quick Target run. See Video Equipment Recommendations.

RedCarpetAcademy.org

LIGHTS, CAMERA
ACTION

Noisy Tripods

Always use a tripod that will not make any noise.

If you hear noise when you are tilting and panning the tripod,

your camera will pick it up.

Scratching. It created an entire genre in the 80s; it was the foundation for hip hop. However, you don't want your video to sound like a RUN-DMC live recording. Make sure your tripod doesn't make a sound.

LIGHTS, CAMERA ACTION

Spare Camera Options

Having a spare camera on hand is essential, but it doesn't have to be an expensive one. Using a less expensive HD camera or even a smart phone as a spare is fine.

"An individual's self-concept is the core of his personality. It affects every aspect of human behavior: the ability to learn, the capacity to grow and change. A strong, positive self-image is the best possible preparation for success in life."

-Dr. Joyce Brothers

LIGHTS, CAMERA ACTION

Fast Pans And Zooms

When you pan and zoom, avoid moving too quickly.

Make your movements slow and smooth.

"One should really use the camera as though tomorrow you'd be stricken blind."
-Dorothea Lange

LIGHTS, CAMERA ACTION

Use A Tripod

Shaky video is distracting and unprofessional.

You want to keep the video steady and the best way to

do that is to use a tripod.

"Hollywood's a mecca, but it's not the final answer. You pick up a camera anyplace in the world, you can make a movie."
-Robert Duvall

68

The Picture ~Perfect Shot~

70

LIGHTS, CAMERA
ACTION

Frame The Shot

When filming a person, make sure that you have some head room.

A good rule of thumb is to have at least a hand's width

of space above the subject's head.

"A film is never really good unless the camera is an eye in the head of a poet."
-Orson Welles

LIGHTS, CAMERA ACTION

Stay Within The Frame

If you are going to be moving around, find out how far

you can move without leaving the frame.

"I like to know where the camera is."
-Jeff Bridges

LIGHTS. CAMERA ACTION

Rule Of Thirds

Avoid placing your subject directly in the center of the frame.

Instead, place them slightly to the side.

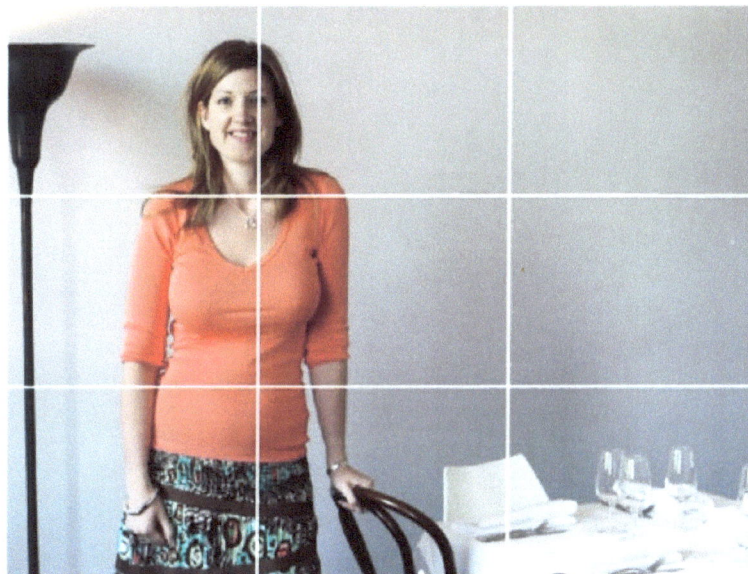

"Hitchcock makes it very clear to us. There's an objective and a subjective camera, like there's a third- and a first-person narrator in literature."
-Manuel Puig

LIGHTS, CAMERA ACTION

The Camera Is Always On

When you are filming, always assume that the camera is rolling. Do not do anything you don't want on camera, such as cursing or scratching.

"Pick up a camera. Shoot something. No matter how small, no matter how cheesy, no matter whether your friends and your sister star in it. Put your name on it as director. Now you're a director. Everything after that you're just negotiating your budget and your fee."

-James Cameron

LIGHTS, CAMERA ACTION

Fix Errors At The Scene

Do your best to prevent and fix most errors while you are filming.

Many things cannot be fixed in post, such as blurry images

and poor audio.

You know how people say "oh, we'll just fix it in post?" Well, editors are not miracle workers, and they can't fix everything. And even if they can fix it, sometimes the fix will be time and cost consuming. So do your absolute best to avoid problems, and fix your errors while you are still filming.

LIGHTS, CAMERA ACTION

Don't Panic

If things seem to be going awry, stay calm. It's not uncommon

for things to go wrong during a shoot, and panicking doesn't help.

Keep calm and try to find the best possible solution,

even if it means rescheduling the shoot.

"There is no panic you can't allay, no problem you can't solve."
-Lauren Weisberger

LIGHTS, CAMERA ACTION

Tilt, Pan, & Zoom

Only use tilts, pans, and zooms when it is necessary.

They become distracting when used too often.

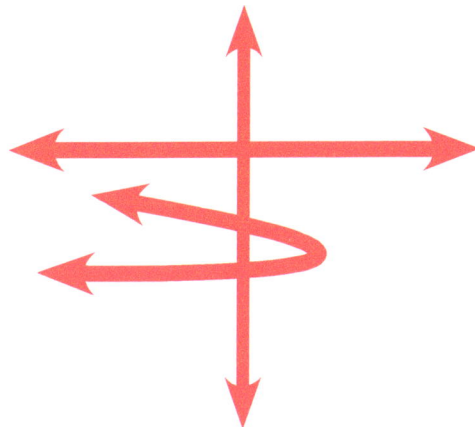

Did you get nauseous while watching the *Blair Witch Project*? 90 minutes of shaky video, panning screens, and instant zooms. I felt like I had spent a day on the tilt-o-whirl. Please don't do this to your viewers. If you do tilt, pan, or zoom, do so slowly and smoothly. The preferred method when you're not using a tripod is to physically move the camera closer to the subject.

LIGHTS, CAMERA ACTION

Film At Your Subject's Height

You want to keep your camera at the same height as your subject,

unless you are filming for a dramatic effect,

as this appears more natural.

"My college degree was in theater. But the real reason, if I have any success in that milieu, so to speak, is because I spent a lot of years directing, I spent a lot of years behind the camera."

-Alton Brown

LIGHTS, CAMERA
ACTION

Check Your Focus

Before you begin recording, make sure that your subject is

in focus. You don't want to film a great take only to find that your

subject is blurry.

Do you want to make your audience feel like they need glasses? No? Then make sure that you've checked your focus so your viewers don't needlessly call their optometrists. Plus, this will distinguish your videos from Uncle Earl's.

     RedCarpetAcademy.org

B-Roll

Be sure to get secondary footage, known as b-roll, of things

like people or locations. You can use this footage over a voiceover

or within the introduction.

"My advice to young film-makers is this: Don't follow trends, Start them!"
-Frank Capra

80

LIGHTS, CAMERA ACTION

More Than One Take

Always have more than one good take to give yourself

some variety when editing.

If you mess up, pick yourself up and try again... after you take a deep breath. This will enable your editor to keep the quality snippets from your audio. Your natural break will provide them the space needed to cut and paste.

LIGHTS, CAMERA
ACTION

Space To Cut

When filming, have a second or two of footage before and after

the subject begins to speak to give the editors space to cut.

You know how you have margins in documents so you have space to cut the paper if you need to? Well, editors like to have a little extra space at the beginning and end of the video so they can cut as well. So film an extra couple of seconds for the poor editor, please!

LIGHTS, CAMERA ACTION

Sunlight

When shooting outdoors, keep the sun behind you.

I know we said NO backlighting, but this is different. When shooting in the great outdoors keep the sun behind you. The last thing we want to see on camera is you squinting. Even Katherine Hepburn couldn't pull off looking good while squinting.

Three-Point Lighting

When possible, try to use a three-point lighting set-up: one light on the subject and two on the set. Also try to turn off any extra artificial lights.

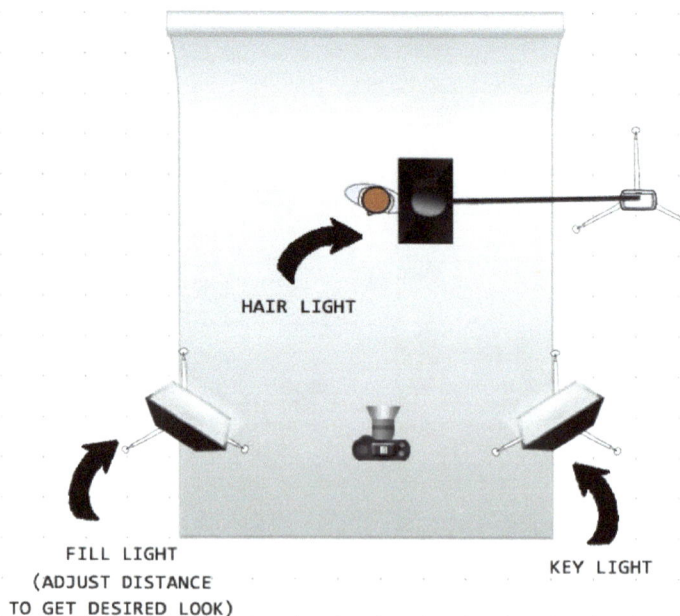

HAIR LIGHT

FILL LIGHT
(ADJUST DISTANCE
TO GET DESIRED LOOK)

KEY LIGHT

"I believe money and celebrity only reveals what is broken and puts it on display for all to see."
— Suzette Hinton

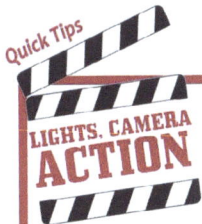

Use A Variety Of Shots

A video that has only one type of shot can be boring.

Use more of a variety of shots and angles to make

the video more interesting.

The Sistine Chapel, a wonder of the world, breaks conventional art and rationale. Standing underneath these tall and illustrious paintings will make you feel small, and you can't help but question: "How? How did he do it?" It's not the imagery of the Sistine Chapel that makes it so wondrous, but the angle. I'm not telling you to film upside down, but try to add variety into your shots. Using angles, spacing, and perspective will make your video a wondrous piece of art that captures the audience's attention.

LIGHTS, CAMERA ACTION

White Balance

Always white balance your camera before a shoot and

whenever the lighting changes or you change locations.

Have you ever seen a video where the colors look off, or where the coloring seems to change between scenes? This is likely because the crew didn't white balance their cameras before they shot. So if you want your video to look right, and to have your whites look like white, then white balance your camera.

LIGHTS. CAMERA ACTION

Back-Up Your Footage

Always have a back-up copy of your footage on an external

drive in case something happens to your original copy.

16 GB

ALWAYS SAVE EVERYTHING. We all know that technology is as much of a curse as it is a blessing. I have lost papers, essays, articles, and unfortunately video recordings. Save multiple edits and versions, so if something happens you will always have a backup. And take the time to set up folders for your footage. Trying to find your footage after the fact can be a nightmare.

LIGHTS, CAMERA ACTION

Windows

Try to avoid filming in front of windows. The light coming through can cause them to become overblown. They can also reflect the camera, lights, and crew. For this reason, you also want to be careful filming around mirrors as well.

Hey, remember what we said about backlighting before? The light from windows i no exception to the rules. Also, we don't want the audience to see what's going on behind-the-scenes in your shots. So please, be careful when filming in front of windows and other reflective surfaces.

Visuals

Don't simply have someone speaking to the camera. This is boring.

Provide other visuals such as text, graphics, or demonstrations.

"Television news is like a lightning flash. It makes a loud noise, lights up everything around it, leaves everything else in darkness and then is suddenly gone."

– Hodding Carter

~ Red Carpet Ready ~

Techniques and Tips For Looking Amazing on Video

92

"And the Oscar goes to… Anne Hathaway!" — The camera quickly pans to Anne Hathaway, who looks stunning, yet surprised. She sheds a few tears (how in the heck does she avoid having an ugly crying face?) and then she walks, ever so elegantly, to the glass podium, and even her shoulder blades look perfect in that low-cut backless dress. Her body knows that there are cameras in EVERY corner, and that they better play their part. She steps to the microphone and thanks everyone that has touched her journey, past and present. She was able to say everything she needed in the one minute she was allotted, with every eloquent word spoken before the proverbial musical version of the hook was forced to pull her off stage.

Now, celebrities like Ms. Hathaway are trained and coached to answer questions under pressure, in the spotlight,and on the red carpet. And to look flawless while doing it. Would you, as a business owner, be as cool, calm, and confident on camera? Would you be able to explain your business' goals, in thirty seconds flat? What about the amazing day when the Today Show or KUSI, wants to interview you, *LIVE*, *on camera*? **GASP**! What would you say? How would you sit? And most importantly: how would you do all of your great work justice?

These tips are here to help you learn exactly what to do should your big break come along.

94

~Appearances~

RedCarpetAcademy.org

LIGHTS, CAMERA ACTION This May Be Your Big Break!

Remember, you never know who will see this video.

This may be the opportunity you have been waiting for.

We live in the days of viral video (the good, the bad, and the oh so ugly). Take your work seriously, regardless of whether you are vlogging or being interviewed. You never know how viral your video can go, or who will see it. Whether it is today or thirty years from now; once it is out on the web, you can't erase it. This will be your virtual footprint.

RedCarpetAcademy.org

**LIGHTS, CAMERA
ACTION**

Look Good For The Camera

If you are going to be filmed, be sure to bring some beauty supplies, such as lipstick and eyeliner, so that you can look good for the camera.

"To not be self-conscious of your appearance is huge, and something that I desperately hope to carry into film at some point in my useless life - to not be thinking, 'My ear looks weird from this angle, why is the camera over there?"

-Anna Kendrick

LIGHTS, CAMERA ACTION

Emergency Beauty Kit

Keep an emergency beauty kit for video purposes. This kit should at least contain the following: lipstick, eyeliner, foundation, moisturizer, hydrating mist, and a make-up brush.

So, you're at an event, and suddenly you've been asked to give a testimonial or give an interview. What a great opportunity! But you don't have the time to go home and fix up your appearance for the camera! This is why you bring an emergency beauty kit. See Beauty Kit Must Haves for suggestions.

RedCarpetAcademy.org

Body Language

Do not slouch or lean backward.

If you are sitting, sit straight up and cross your ankles.

If you are standing, stand with your feet about hips distance apart.

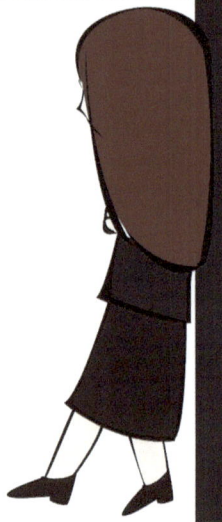

My grandmother epitomizes class. At age 86, her posture is statuesque. She even crosses her legs when she is being chauffeured around the city (by myself). It's no wonder that I would get chastised for slouching, smacking, blowing bubbles with my gum, tapping my fingers, and the absolute worst: sitting without my legs crossed. The next time you are being interviewed, imagine that my grandmother is sitting across from you, scrutinizing your every move. Proper posture will give you an air of confidence; so sit up, cross your legs, and exude elegance.

LIGHTS. CAMERA ACTION

Hair

Smooth hair looks best on camera. So keep some hairspray

and a brush or comb on hand to keep your hair tame.

Yikes! You don't want to look like you've received a static shock do you? Tame those flyaways down, and go on camera with smooth hair.

Clothing Patterns

Try to avoid wearing clothing with stripes, checks, or small patterns.

They often do not come out very well in video.

Solid colors. That electric paisley suit was made for Studio 54 not NBC 7.

LIGHTS, CAMERA
ACTION

Powder: To Use Or Not To Use

Avoid using powder for HD video shoots as it sits on

top of the skin and gives off a scaly look.

Liza Minnelli. Icon known for her full face of makeup and chain of ex-husbands. Liza Minelli's pounds of foundation can be seen from outer-space. Now imagine what it must look like in high definition; you can witness the line formations on her face from her excessive makeup. Ladies, you don't want this to be you and gentlemen, think Liberace. Ease up on the powder, because HD means they will see EVERYTHING. Be minimal.

LIGHTS, CAMERA ACTION

Shiny Faces

A shiny face can appear nervous, untrustworthy, or lacking confidence.

Use a mist and a make-up brush to give off a translucent look.

"I have the insecurities of any actress, I suppose of any woman. Even the most beautiful ones feel unhappy. Look at Bardot: she was suicidal. But I like to play with the camera. I like to ham it up."

-Chloe Sevigny

104

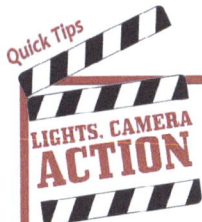

Ready For The Media?

If you are going to be attending an event that the media may be

attending, be sure to bring your emergency beauty kit.

"I certainly never expected to be in front of a camera one day of my life."
-Jennifer Garner

Whiter, Brighter Smile

Use whitening strips for whiter, brighter smile, as this

cannot be fixed in video like it can be in photos.

Yellow is such a beautiful color. It's a great color choice for your new baby's room, sundress, or tie. The only context it looks terrible in are teeth. We want your pearly whites to show and if that requires bleach, then whitening strips here we come!

106

LIGHTS, CAMERA ACTION

Smile

Be careful what emotions you are expressing while on camera, because they will be amplified. Keep a simple, neutral smile; you want to look like an approachable person with something interesting to say.

"You can always tell folks from nonfolks. Folks like to feel good, like to smile for the camera when there's a big photo opportunity for a really good cause."
-Russell Baker

107

108

~Interviewing~

110

LIGHTS, CAMERA ACTION

Interviewing

If you plan on interviewing people, be sure to have your set of questions ready before you begin the interview. It is always best to do a trial run with the interviewee beforehand.

1. Who are you? What do you do?

2. What does your product/service do?

3. How did you come up with the idea for the product service?

4. Why should people buy the product/ use the service?

"Being an entrepreneur is a mindset. You have to see things as opportunities all the time. I like to do interviews. I like to push people on certain topics. I like to dig into the stories where there's not necessarily a right or wrong answer."

-Soledad O'Brien

LIGHTS, CAMERA ACTION

Find A Quiet Spot For Interviews

If you are pulled aside for an interview, make sure that they place you in a spot that is quiet and doesn't have a blank wall behind you. Also make sure that objects behind you, such as plants, don't appear odd in the frame.

Have you watched a video or something on TV, and there is a lot of background noise? It distracts from the message, doesn't it? If using a camera mic, make sure the camera is pointing away from the loud noises if you can't avoid them entirely. This will at least dull the noise. An even better solution: wear a lapel and use an external camera mic to have two audio channels. See Video Equipment Recommendations.

Warm-Up The Interview

When interviewing a person, warm them up with the easier

questions; leave the hardest questions for the end.

This is not the Spanish Inquisition, well perhaps your interview is, which is fine (ehem, Barbara Walters), but give your interviewee time to breathe and warm up to you. The better the relationship between the two of you, the more enthused they will feel to share personal information.

~The Audience~

Know Your Audience

In order to choose the right style and pace for your video, you need to know who your audience is, and what is most likely to call out to them.

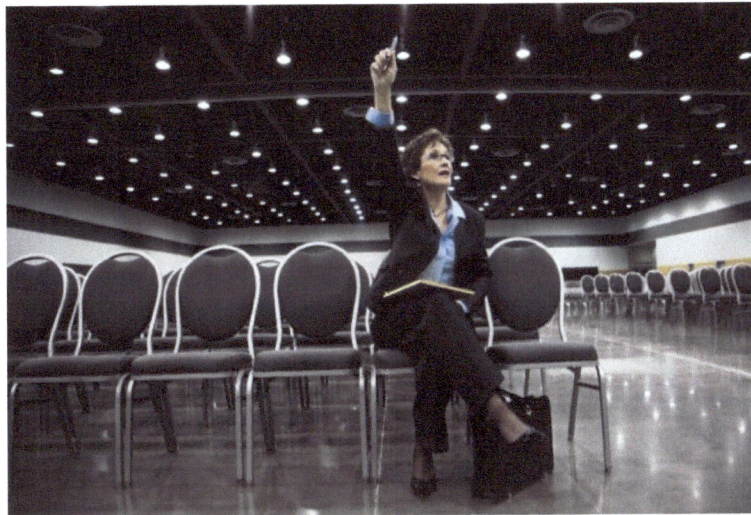

Your tone, range, pitch, and style is contingent upon one thing: your audience. Most people think the most important element of a speech or presentation is the content. *FALSE*. It's your audience. Knowing who you are speaking to will shape what you are saying, what's relevant, and how to share your message. For ex: Selling something provocative, like a new line of craft beer? Sharing craft beer with a group of recently retired seniors vs. thirty-year-old artists will be drastically different. Same product but different message.

LIGHTS, CAMERA ACTION

Who Are You Speaking To?

When you are looking at the camera lens, think about who you are talking to. This way, you are not looking blankly at the camera and your audience believes that you are speaking directly to them.

"I'm always aware of the camera and it feels like that's the audience."
-Alan Rickman

LIGHTS, CAMERA ACTION

Make It About Them

*You may be the expert and have a message to share, but remember: no one likes to be talked **at**. Making your message about the audience first will create greater engagement, lead to more sales and build longer lasting relationships with your customers, potential customers and viewers.*

Remember your college Physics professor? He stood there with his elbow patched tweed jacket, with wireless glasses on the tip of his nose, explaining the complexities of the universe, but it sounded more like a 90 minute lecture affirming that you will never be as intelligent as he is? Don't be that person. Your goal is to ensure that people understand your product/good/service. Use common terms, analogies, and metaphors; ensure that your audience will have a profound understanding of what you do by the time you are done speaking.

LIGHTS, CAMERA ACTION

Statistics

Statistics can help you emphasize your point and keep the audience's attention. "One in five women suffer from stage fright" is much more effective than "A large number of women suffer from stage fright."

Numbers don't lie, or so say our politicians. In this case, sharing statistics gives credibility to your point, plus it tells your audience that you did your research.

LIGHTS, CAMERA ACTION

Storyline Format

Don't assume that your audience knows a lot about your subject.

Use a storyline format. Have a clear beginning, middle, and end.

Share your subject as if you are describing it for the first time. Back in the day, telemarketers would leave messages starting in the middle of a sentence. This tactic worked well for those people to return calls. After all, no one likes to feel left out or as if they didn't hear correctly. However, the public is savvier than before. Don't do it.

~ Media Ready ~

RedCarpetAcademy.org

LIGHTS, CAMERA ACTION

Know Your Hook

When giving your story to the media, create a tie-in with a newsworthy story. Ask yourself why someone would want to feature your story. Finding a legitimate connection to a hot topic will greatly increase your chances of getting coverage.

If your local news has been covering multiple segments on the military and your piece fits in, pitch it. The media has to hunt for relevant content and if you have something that they could use, you are essentially delivering them a beautiful Christmas package with a golden bow.

LIGHTS. CAMERA. ACTION

Pitch The Media

Don't be afraid to approach the media. They need your story

as much as you need them to tell it.

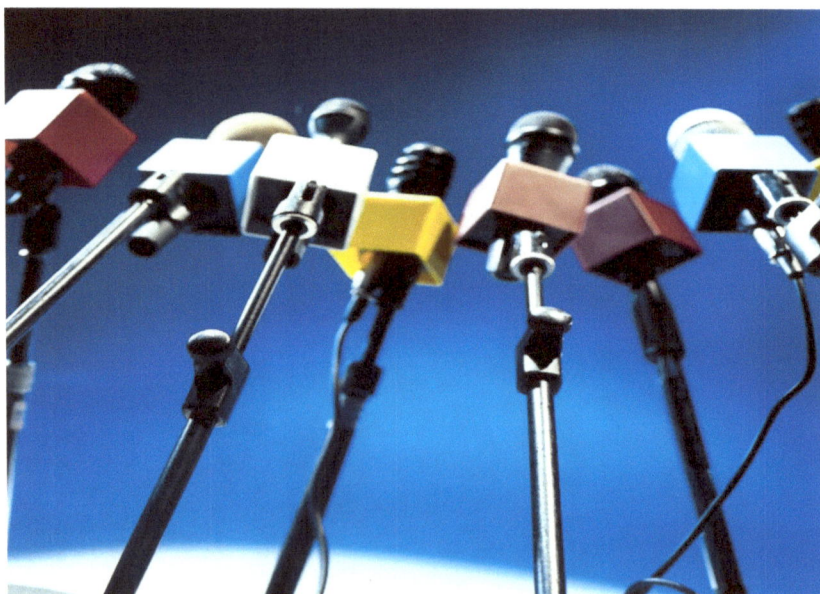

The media is not Jake Ryan in *16 Candles* and YOU are not that awkward red-headed girl (Molly Ringwald) hoping that he will pay attention to you. Remember, the only way he noticed her, was due to the note she dropped in study hall? Even Molly Ringwald made a pitch. Don't be shy, put yourself out there and share your message with the media. They are continuously looking for content, so you are doing them a favor.

LIGHTS. CAMERA
ACTION

Repurpose Your Video

You can, and should, reuse clips that you have created in multiple projects. From making longer or shorter versions of the original video to making short clips to send to clients.

If you are just starting out with your video channel, it may seem daunting to have to create more than one video. This is why you keep all footage, and catalog what type of footage it is, for instance: events, personal interviews, vlogs, network interviews, etc. This gives you lots of clips to choose from, and you will be on your way to sharing more than one video.

LIGHTS, CAMERA ACTION

Memorization

Even if you are using a teleprompter, it is still a

good idea to practice and memorize a list of talking points.

"I like figuring out where I need to be mentally so that I'm not thinking about the camera and that it's second nature. I want to get to a place where I can exist within the confines of what you can do with filmmaking and not have to think about it."

-Anna Kendrick

128

Be Energetic!

Low-energy performances tend to lose the audience's attention.

You want to keep their focus on YOU!

"An energetic man will succeed where an indolent one would vegetate and inevitably perish."

-Jules Verne

LIGHTS. CAMERA ACTION

Use Your Nerves

If you are nervous, channel that nervous energy into something

productive. Use the energy to put more emphasis into your performance.

"I think that I need to work on being comfortable at being normal, everyday-ish on camera. Unlike a lot of actors, I think that's the thing that I'm not so comfortable with."

-Christina Ricci

LIGHTS. CAMERA ACTION

Avoid Rambling

Try to stay on topic and get to the point quickly.

Otherwise you risk losing your audience.

Blah...blah... blah...blah....

VS

This is the point of my topic

Are you a type A personality that you wish most people would just get to the point? Or maybe have a Chatty Kathy in the family? Less is more. Keep to the point.

LIGHTS, CAMERA ACTION

Own The Space

Your body is occupying space. You fill that space not only with your physical body, but with your wisdom, knowledge, and personality. So when you speak, take ownership of your expertise and the relationship with your audience. Don't just occupy the space, own it!

The coined phrase, "My space, your space" is not applicable in this instance. When on camera, it is all your space. Not physically, but with confidence.

LIGHTS. CAMERA ACTION

Should I Eat?

You should eat something at least 60-90 minutes before going on set or onstage so that your stomach isn't growling and you don't feel lightheaded. Be careful what you eat, though. Try sticking to healthy options that will give you energy.

Scarlett O'Hara made fainting oh-so romantic. However, this isn't *Gone with the Wind II*. Make sure you are hydrated and have eaten prior to filming, so you will enrapture the camera vertically, as opposed to horizontally, while you lay face down, bum up in the air. Also, having even a snack will ensure that the lapel doesn't capture your growling stomach. It's not very appealing unless you're in comedy skit.

Foods To Avoid

You should avoid food that takes a long time to digest, drys your mouth, gets stuck in your teeth, impairs your judgement, gives you gas, or makes you feel bloated. You should avoid the following before a shoot: heavy meals, beans, coffee, berries, alcohol, and spicy foods.

What do you eat before a 5k? A double cheeseburger with bacon? Or an extra large pepperoni pizza? I think not. Presenting requires great energy, just like a race. Choose foods that will fuel you through the presentation but don't send you into a grease-infused food coma.

Preventing Dry Mouth

Keep apple slices nearby. A piece of apple does a better job of keeping your mouth from drying out than just water.

"You don't want to keep giving yourself a sugar spike and then crash and get exhausted and need coffee because you shoot for a long time. On set, I eat a lot of peanut butter and apples, things that have actual energy and protein in them to keep me going."

-Allison Williams

RedCarpetAcademy.org

136

~Spectacular Selfies~

Techniques and Tips For Amazing Photos

RedCarpetAcademy.org

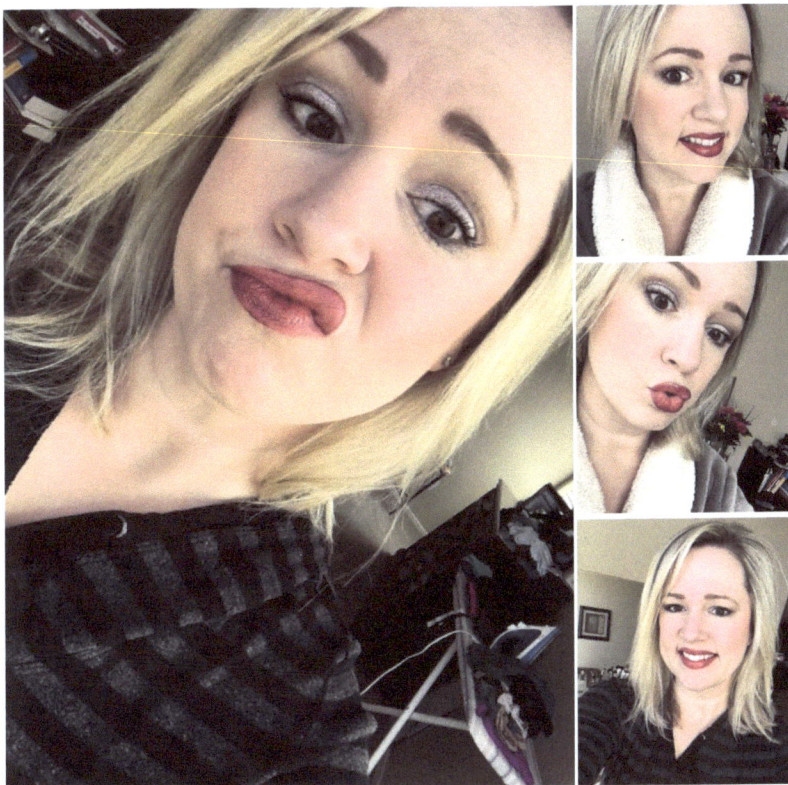

Photography by: Christine Brainard Smith

According to her Instagram™ page, Kendell Jenner has over 43 million followers on Instagram™. Some say she is able to keep and build her followers by being the "Selfie Queen."

"I'm a very loyal and very private person when it comes to my personal life. But I obviously do have Twitter™ and Instagram™, and I will share some of the things I'm doing."

-*Kendall Jenner*

LIGHTS, CAMERA ACTION

The Right Lighting

Try posing in a place that has beautiful lighting. Great lighting can equal an amazing selfie! The magic hours (the hour after sunrise and the hour after sunset) often have the best lighting.

"Light makes photography. Embrace light. Admire it. Love it. But above all, know light. Know it for all you are worth, and you will know the key to photography."
-George Eastman

LIGHTS. CAMERA ACTION

Framing Your Picture

The Rule of Thirds applies to selfies as well! Posing with your head in the upper left or right corners of the frame can help make your selfie look interesting.

"To me, photography is an art of observation. It's about finding something interesting in an ordinary place... I've found it has little to do with the things you see and everything to do with the way you see them."

-Elliott Erwitt

LIGHTS, CAMERA ACTION

Learn Your Settings

Play with the setting on your phone's camera. Playing with things like the exposure, focus, and effects can add some 'oomph' to your selfie.

"Photography, as a powerful medium of expression and communications, offers an infinite variety of perception, interpretation and execution."
-Ansel Adams

RedCarpetAcademy.org

**LIGHTS, CAMERA
ACTION**

Look Natural

Don't force it! Pose in a way that feels natural to you.

And express yourself! Smile, frown, pout; show some emotion!

It makes a better photo.

"Photography is a way of feeling, of touching, of loving. What you have caught on film is captured forever... it remembers little things, long after you have forgotten everything."

-Aaron Siskind

Play With Angles

Have some fun with your angles. Turn your head to the left and right to find your best side. It looks better than straight-on shots. Also, angles from above tend to look best in selfies.

"To me, photography is an art of observation. It's about finding something interesting in an ordinary place... I've found it has little to do with the things you see and everything to do with the way you see them."

-Elliott Erwitt

LIGHTS. CAMERA
ACTION

Practice, Practice, Practice

Like many other things, practice does indeed make perfect.

Try to find some time to practice taking pictures, and play with

angles, expressions, and camera settings.

"My father taught me that the only way you can make good at anything is to practice, and then practice some more."

-Pete Rose

But Most of All...

Make sure you're having fun!

"Just keep taking chances and having fun."
-Garth Brooks

148

~ *Bonus Tips* ~

Tips Directly From Our Experts To Help You Be Camera Ready!

How to Receive Google Juice and Optimize with Videos

5 DIY Tips: Promotion is Key

With so many business-related videos on YouTube and those other "viral" videos competing for attention, and more being added every day, you need to put some effort in it if you want your brand and story to stand out.

Five quick tips to help you create your YouTube channel with the power of a YouTube presence.

Tip #1: Reinforce who you are (Call to Action)

At the end of every company video you upload to YouTube, remember to reinforce your brand and a call to action. For example, you could say your company name and web address at the end of each clip and add Call Today or For More Information. Include an image showing this information in the final frame of your video with your photo if you are the brand. If you fail to do this, people might forget who you are by the end, depending on the length of the video they've just watched.

Tip #2: Add your social media links (Make your channel easy to subscribe or share)

Your YouTube channel shouldn't be treated as an individual online entity. It's definitely a good idea to include your other social media links within the channel. For example, if people like your video and what you've had to say, they might want to follow you on Twitter or Facebook.

Tip #3: Take time choosing your avatar

The avatar for your YouTube channel is also an important consideration. You need to bear in mind that you're competing with millions of other company video channels, so an eye-catching logo that stands out for all the right reasons is essential.

Tip #4: Add your logo to your videos in a subtle way

A watermarked logo can be added to your videos in a subtle way so that people are aware of it without it being intrusive. This also helps with branding if other people decide to embed your video on their websites.

Tip #5: Include your brand in the tags

Include your company name/brand name as the final tag when you're adding these for each video you upload. If you put this at the beginning, you're using up a valuable space that should feature one of your main keywords.

Including your brand is great if you've recorded a series of videos and want the others to be displayed as related content. And don't forget those hash tags # to spread the love.

10 Tips to Engage Any Audience

By Jenn Kaye

1. Own the Space

Whether you are speaking live in front of an audience or on-camera, there is a space that your body occupies. You fill that space with not only your physical presence, but your wisdom, your knowledge and your personality.

When you speak, take ownership of the expertise you have to share and the relationship with your audience. Just because you may only be speaking for 5 minutes or 50, don't just rent the space, own it.

2. Smile

When you're onstage, or on-camera, it doesn't matter what kind of day you're having and if all you feel like doing is growling at anyone you have to speak to.

A smile conveys warmth, welcome, confidence and joy. It draws people to you like a magnet and gives you the freedom to talk about any topic – because ultimately it builds trust, rapport and approachability.

3. Let Go of Perfection

If you're anything like me, you *love* for everything to be just perfect. Here's the deal. At the end of the day, there is *no such place* as "perfect." Your audience wants to know they can trust you, that you understand who they are, what their challenges are and where they're coming from. They're not interested in the perfection.

They want to know you're human. If your hair doesn't look perfect on camera, or the sound system goes out, don't let the imperfection distract you from the most important part – sharing your message and connecting with your audience.

4. Be Real

Again, whether your audience is live in front of you or viewing you from a recorded video, people can tell when we are trying to be someone we're not. Think about it, you know when someone is being genuine don't you? There is a way that they stand, a tone to their voice, the way their eyes connect with you and a way that they speak that makes you either connect with them or roll your eyeballs and start critiquing their lack of authenticity.

When you think about the people that are most "real" to you, what is it about them that makes you feel that way?

More often than not, they are willing to share stories that show their vulnerability, their silly side, that share something personal about their life, their kids, their relationships or their experiences.

Authenticity and vulnerability creates engagement. Be willing to get uncomfortable and speak from your whole self.

5. Be Ready for the Unexpected

There will always be unexpected challenges that come up when you are speaking or filming. I remember a time when I was working with an entertainment company and performing for a group of 500 businessmen.

The sound went out in the middle of our first number, we lost not only the sound for the band but the sound on the mic, and to top things off, the velcro on my Can-Can skirt (yes, I said Can-Can skirt...) started to come undone and I had quite simply two choices: I could 1) Completely freak out with the all the unexpected challenges and take the focus away from the show by throwing a hissy fit or 2) I could incorporate it all into the show and improvise.

If the unexpected can throw you off when you are presenting, it's time to do a little troubleshooting. Taking either an improv class or on-camera class is perfect for helping you not only feel more comfortable, it's great for building your what-do-I-do-now-that-everything-has-gone-completely-wonky confidence and use the unexpected as opportunities to go even deeper in your connection with your audience.

6. Love Your Voice

The single greatest critic in our lives is US. Often if we don't like something about ourselves (our voice, our hair, our drooping eye, the way we sound when we're talking) it comes out in our presentation. We allow our inner critic to prevent us from creating real engagement with our audience, because instead of being present to them in the moment, we are busy with the background noise in our heads criticizing every little detail.

Love your voice means to not only love the way you sound and embrace the way you speak, it also means to love the content or information you're sharing.

You have a unique voice. A message that only you can share. Don't compare yourself to anyone else who you think is doing something similar. Love *your voice* and your audience will love you too.

7. Speak From Your Heart, Not Your Head

It takes tremendous courage to be yourself, and to speak from the place of who you truly are versus who you think you're supposed to be.

When we speak from our heart, there is a different vibration or rhythm that occurs. Our tone of voice changes and we become more grounded in our body. When we speak from our heart, there is a natural alignment that occurs that creates a natural connection and deeper engagement with our audience or listeners.

When you speak from your heart, there's very little need for notes or a script. Because what's true is simply true and you know it within the deepest core of your being. When you speak from your heart it simply feels *easy*. When you're speaking from your head you tend to worry more about the details and if you missed one section or another.

Speak from your heart and you will create instant rapport with your audience every time.

8. Use Your Whole Body to Communicate

Let's be honest, we've seen people speaking or have seen their videos where they just look like a talking head. There's no *movement*. They seem stiff, like they're completely uncomfortable and as if they're not even enjoying this experience speaking with you.

The thing is, when it comes to interacting with others, 55% of all our communication is based in our non-verbal body language which includes: facial expressions, hand gestures, eye contact and posture. We could actually tell an entire story without saying one single word, simply by using our whole body to communicate.

When you're onstage, use your whole body to tell a story and convey your message.

When you're on-camera, keep your feet planted but use your hands and facial expressions to tell your story. (If you move your feet on camera you may just walk right out of the shot! Besides, it's also completely distracting and communicates to the viewer that you are uncertain of yourself.)

9. Practice the Power of the Pause™

I was taking an Argentine Tango class one weekend, and the instructor was explaining how after each movement you bring your feet together and pause, so that you can actually reconnect with your partner and know where you are going to move together next.

What really hit home was this: that so often when we are connected with another person (or our audience or viewers) and we are constantly moving, we can become disconnected. The pause allows us to re-establish our connection, make sure we are still engaged together and move forward *together*, instead of leaving them behind.

When you are speaking, try not to rush through your content. I know it can be tempting to want to say everything and squeeze it all in, but sometimes less is more. Take the time to speak slowly and make each point count.

10. Make Your Message About *Them*

Yes, you are the expert. And yes, you may have a message to share, a story to tell, something to teach. However, no one likes to be talked *at*.

Jeffrey Gitomer, the #1 Sales Authority in the U.S. says repeatedly, "People don't like to be sold, but they love to buy." When speaking it is a similar mantra. People don't like to be lectured, chided, criticized, spoken down to or made to feel less-than. People DO like to feel important, like you care, that you understand them and can relate.

Make them feel like they are the most important person in the world. And in that moment, they are.

Keep in mind that especially as women, we do business with people we know, like and trust. Be sure when sharing your message you translate your experience, your sales offer or your content to be audience-centric rather than ego-centric. Making your message about them first will create greater engagement, lead to more sales and build longer lasting relationships with your customers, potential customers and viewers.

Jenn Kaye

Master the Language of Communication™

Jenn Kaye is a Master Communicator, Language Expert, and Keynote Speaker whose contagious enthusiasm adds a refreshing spark to everyday challenges. Through her corporate trainings, facilitation, and high-impact keynote presentations, Jenn has emerged as a relevant voice and progressive thought leader on the art of communication. Engaging, real, and insightful, Jenn delivers intentional and customized, high-content programs for your audiences with bite-size wisdom they can implement immediately.

Phone: 480.422.5433

Website: jennkaye.com

Email: jenn@jennkaye.com

LinkedIn: linkedin.com/in/jennkaye

Facebook: facebook.com/jennkaye

Twitter: @jennkaye

10 Things to Look for During a Photo Shoot

By Natalia Robert

1. Smile and let your personality show and try as much as possible so you don't look like you're faking it.

2. Relax and chill out. Just go with the flow, as the photographer will be assisting you to get the best pictures possible. If you feel your photo shoot is getting overwhelming, take deep breaths before resuming.

3. Keep your body as natural as possible: tilt your head a few degrees to avoid looking stiff.

4. Pose with a relaxed appearance so your body language shows off your personality.

5. Don't let your arms touch your body, otherwise they will get flattened and look bigger than they actually are.

6. As for a sitting pose, project your body slightly forward.

7. Don't look straight into the camera. Instead, bend your head a bit and let your eyes look at the lens.

8. Avoid looking at the lights to keep them from damaging your eyes.

9. Keep the joints flowing naturally but avoid overextending them.

10. Use different emotions and expressions that complement the concept to create some versatility.

Natalia Robert
Founder of Full Circle Images

Natalia has been photographing life for over 15 years and is bringing her unique eye to spaces and businesses all over Southern California. Her world travels, love of the outdoors, and fun energy blend perfectly for a memorable photo session that is tailor-made to each client. Her years in architecture and graphic arts, meanwhile, bring a keen design eye to all final images. While Natalia is always happy behind a camera, she especially enjoys photographing beautiful homes, as well as collaborating with fellow local business owners to refine their branding images.

Phone: 858.255.0855

Website: fcisandiego.com

Email: natalia@fcisandiego.com

Instagram: @fullcircleimages

Facebook: facebook.com/fullcircleimages

Twitter: @presetparadise

Customize Your Sound Bite

By Felena Hanson

1. Your elevator pitch should include things such as your name and business, but more importantly, it needs to focus on benefits. "What's in it for me? What are you going to do for me?"

2. An analogy can help give people an idea of what your business is like by using a comparison to something completely outside of your industry that is easily recognizable. So whenever you are doing something a little different, using an analogy can really help your audience understand it.

3. If you are a founder or a creator, mention it. Too many people glaze over this fairly important detail that the audience should know.

4. Focus on what makes you different. There are likely a lot of people who do the same basic thing you do, so what separates you from them? How do you stand out?

5. Be sure to end with a zinger. Have a tagline that the audience will easily remember.

6. It is much easier to get perspective from other people. Have someone you know, but don't know well, help you work on your pitch and find what stands out about your business.

7. Don't try to be the same or similar to your competitors. You want to stand out.

8. Make sure that your message leaves an impact. It needs to be meaningful to your target audience.

9. Make it short and sweet. You only have a short period of time to impress your audience.

10. What you want to think about as well is "how does this come out on video" and "how are you building a connection with your audience immediately."

Felena Hanson

Founder of Hera Hub

Felena is a long-time entrepreneur and marketing maven. Her latest venture, Hera Hub, is a spa-inspired shared workspace for female entrepreneurs. This as-needed, flexible work and meeting space provides a productive environment for women who primarily work from home. Hera Hub members have access to a professional space to meet with clients and to connect and collaborate with like-minded business owners, thus giving them the support they need to be prosperous. Cost-effective monthly membership options are suited for freelancers, independent consultants, entrepreneurs, nonprofits, and authors.

Felena is passionate about education, earning her Bachelor's degree in Marketing from the University of San Diego and her MBA from California State University Dominguez Hills.

HERA HUB
WORKSPACE FOR WOMEN

Phone: 619.889.7852

Website: herahub.com

Email: felena@herahub.com

LinkedIn: linkedin.com/in/felenahanson

Facebook: facebook.com/herahub

Twitter: @herahub

Zen Media inc.

Media Training Tips For Entrepreneurs

By Angela Chee

The Interview

Have a media interview, but nervous about what to say or how to say it? Here are a few Zen tips to make sure you are confident and prepared.

1. **Before your interview, make sure you define your key messages**. These are the most important points you want to get across during your interview. Make a list of some brief messages that can be stated in 15 seconds or less. Know what you want to communicate and convey them in "sound bites" -good quotes.

2. **Be brief and stay on point.** Remember your key messages and know that reporters only use one or two eight second "sound bites." Make your words count. If there is only one message, say it several times in different ways.

3. **Listen to the question before responding.** Don't get distracted. Make sure you know what question you are answering.

4. **Stay in control of the interview.** Make sure you present your key messages in the beginning, even if the interviewer doesn't ask the question.

5. **Image is important.** Dress for the audience, but always look professional and polished. Bright solid colors look best. If wearing a dark suit, accent with colorful blouse or tie. Do not wear anything distracting, striped, loud prints, or jewelry.

The Pitch

Whether you get news coverage depends on how you pitch your story. While there is no one "right" way to convey your message, there are ways to help make sure you are heard and get on the air.

1. **Make sure you have the right contact.** You don't want to leave a message on a general voicemail box. Find someone you can pitch or get the correct e-mail address. It can be a reporter, an assignment editor, booker, or a producer.

2. **Don't just send a press release.** Attach the press release for additional details, but make sure you write a specific short pitch at the top.

3. **Know your hook.** Create a tie-in with your service or product with a newsworthy story. Ask yourself, why would anyone care about the story? What makes the story interesting? Why would a producer/editor want this story in their show or column? Find a legitimate connection to a hot topic and you can increase your chances of getting coverage.

4. **Provide resources.** Make the reporters/producers job easy. It's not enough to give a story idea; you also need to help them tell the story. Offer to supply the reporter with background information, interviews, sources, and video/photo opportunities. Be specific.

5. **Know the right time and show to pitch.** What type of story is it? Who does it appeal to? A light feature may do better on the weekends when the media outlet is short on stories. Harder news stories are for the evening news. Mid-day news may be good for health, senior, and women's issues. Morning News is good for live interviews.

Angela Chee

Founder of Zen Media Inc.

Angela Chee is a Host, Speaker, Writer and Founder of Zen Media Inc., a media training and consulting company and The Zen Mom.com, an informative and inspirational website for moms. As a former news anchor/reporter with more than 15 years of experience in the broadcast industry, Angela has worked in top TV markets from KCBS/KCAL-TV, and KNBC-TV in Los Angeles to Fox 6 in San Diego. She has hosted shows for networks like E! Entertainment, HGTV (Home and Garden Television), Channel One News and helped launch Entertainment Tonight China.

Her mission is to empower through Wisdom, Inspiration and Laughter. She believes everyone has a story to share and helps people find their voice, communicate effectively and find their "zen" when it comes to promoting their business and brand.

Phone: 310.489.6134

Website: zenmediainc.com

Email: angela@zenmediainc.com

Instagram: @angelacheetv

Facebook: facebook.com/angelacheetv

Twitter: @angelacheetv

Maximize Your Video with Social Media

with Holly Kolman

1. Make a "Videos" section on your website so visitors can find them quickly when they visit your site from social media sites.

2. Add social sharing buttons to your website that show below each post. It's not enough to have one set of "Follow us" buttons in the corner of the site. If you want people to share, make it easy! Your website developer can install software to do this for you.

3. Create and post content in your video that is interesting, funny, controversial, heartstring pulling, and/or genuinely helpful and worth sharing. Often, when want people to get to know our products and services; the message can come across as boring (yes, boring!) because we are focusing only on our own point of view instead of how customers think. If you didn't work for your company, would you want to watch your video for its own sake? If not, rewrite your script and try again.

4. Create short, simple "How To" videos on a subject people want to learn that is in your area of expertise. People will share it if the video is helpful or funny.

5. Create ready-to-use sound bite videos for busy reporters and bloggers that give your opinion about something controversial in your industry. These videos can be used by instantly without taking time to schedule an interview.

6. Add a short "For more information" screen at the end of your video with social media symbols next to your username for each social media site.

7. Write interesting, keyword-rich headlines for your videos to make people curious to watch them whey they are posted on social media sites.

8. People on social media have short attention spans, so share short videos. Two minutes is an average time for a viral video, and shorter is better.

9. Try joining private groups on Facebook, LinkedIn, Google and Yahoo. You can post your video to the group so people who are interested in your topic can see it. Keep it relevant to the purpose of the group.

10. Privately ask influencers you know to share your video. This can be done with a private message, email, text or phone call. Let them know why you think it would interest their followers and don't overpitch – keep your request low key, and you might find yourself out in front of a whole new audience.

Holly Kolman

Digital Marketing Consultant

Holly Kolman has a brain like a computer and a heart for people. Holly's sites have outranked Disney, Hertz, and Nordstrom on Google, and she prides herself on gaining clarity of ideas and writing for humans while at the same time giving search engines what they want.

Holly makes Twitter make sense for people who find it overwhelming. A technology early adopter, Holly was building made-for-mobile websites before the first iPhone came to market and an avid Twitter user before it went mainstream.

Additionally, she was a finalist and won the popular vote for Blogger of the Year in the InfluenceSD Champions of New Media competition and won an Excellence in Health Care Public Relations award in Chicago.

Website: mobileholly.com

Email: holly@mobileholly.com

LinkedIn: linkedIn.com/in/hollykolman

Twitter: @mobileholly

Equipment Tips

by Anita Miranda

1. Learn what type of camera you have, it's functions, and know your camera settings.

2. Become familiar with your tripod. Know how tall your tripod is and make sure it's for video and not for photography. Always level the head after mounting the camera.

3. Check your audio sound. Use external microphones to get better audio. Headphones are the best way to test your audio.

4. Batteries: charge all batteries the night before and have at least two extra batteries, plus take your power supply and your charger.

5. Lighting: look for the best light at the location and ask your subjects to stand there. Natural lighting is best unless you are working with a green screen. Shoot with light on someone's face rather than light coming from behind the person.

6. Shoot a lot of footage; the more the better you have to choose footage. Always have at least two solid takes. Check your test video shot first. Make sure your camera is recording, audio is clean, and your talent is sharp and framed correctly before continuing.

7. Have two SD Cards that are at least 16 GB and at Ultra Class 10, and format your card in your camera before using each time. Video takes up much more space especially HD. Don't be surprised to have the dreaded message "Disk Full."

8. Add lenses to your camera or even iPhone for a better close-up and more coverage with better video quality.

9. White balance at every location. Either have with you a white posterboard or white-balance cloth.

10. Video cameras cannot be turned sideways like photographs. Also if you have a blurred shot and it is not part of the storyboard, the party is over. There is nothing in the market that can clean up blurred footage or images.

Wardrobe, Hair, Makeup, & Body Works

by Anita Miranda

1. Give yourself a thorough treatment and makeover, a week before the day: facials, eyebrows, should be primed to perfection. If you're generally good to go, a couple of minutes of exfoliation can also be useful to bring out the inner youthfulness from your skin.

2. Most of us neglect this but your digits are important since they get to pose a lot! They should be in natural color and healthy.

3. Most likely you'd be smiling for the camera, so if possible get your teeth whitened as well.

4. A simple hair trimming can do wonders for your picture. Check if you have any split ends or brittle hair.

5. Get plenty of rest a few days before the photo-shoot – you don't want obvious dark circles! Plus tired faces can really show up in the pictures.

6. Drink plenty of water to keep active and the puckers moist.

7. Eat! Stick to healthy foods and no extreme diets to avoid feeling tired during the session.

8. Discuss thoroughly with the photographer on what kind of results you are looking for to avoid any dramatic changes.

9. Read through the concept couple of days beforehand so you can get the feel of what kind of emotions and poses you want to show off.

10. After that, search online for some of the poses suitable for your photo shoot, so your body and mind will be ready for the day, which in turn speeds up the session.

11. Dust exposed skin with a little bit of glitter, shimmer, or bronzer to make your skin hydrated as well as accentuating the features.

12. You can also use a bit of self-tanner sparingly (under arms and calves) to create a toned body.

13. Don't forget; add a lighter color to your pucker area of your lips to keep your lips looking fuller. You may use a creamy lipstick with a dab of Vaseline.

14. Keep your hair healthy and super shiny with Moroccan Oil then use hair spray.

15. Always pick heels as they can elongate your legs (the higher the better, yet comfortable). Always keep a pair of nude heels for those times you need to strike a pose full length. Nothing is worse than cutting your frame in sections with the wrong color shoes. Remember the days of match your purse and your shoes. Those days are long gone. The camera is not kind. You want long and lean.

16. Choose one key accessory but keep the rest simple. For example, grand necklace goes well with a simple ring.

17. While we're on accessories, choose a small and handy purse. We're at an event, not at a supermarket. If needed, keep your emergency kit in another satchel close by.

RedCarpetAcademy.org

18. Pose with confidence: put one hand on hips and smile naturally. Find your mark. Nowadays, there are many camera lenses pointing at the subject. Choose where your want your eyes to be photographed straight on. Or like the pros do, move and pose in various angles including where your eyes are focused on.

19. Don't show your skin more than you need, otherwise you'll look hesitant and not enjoying the night (that will show up in the pictures). Rule of thumb, more cleavage equals little leg, peak-a-boo cleavage equals show-stopping legs.

20. Always stash key items in the purse: mints, needle and thread (with the same color of the dress), Band-Aids, and even bobby pins to be well prepared for any incident.

Anita Miranda

Video Marketing Strategist

If the thought of being photographed, videotaped or interviewed terrifies you, Red Carpet Academy founded and run by Anita Miranda, is just what the doctor ordered. Her business is to make YOU and your business stand out on camera. We live in a digital world with videos, YouTube, Pinterest, vlogging, blogging, posting, holy moly it's all so much. Keeping up with the Jones' can be rather difficult and whatever your reason for keeping your distance it's time to face the music and embrace Video Marketing. Presenting Video Marketing for Entrepenuars and the production agency of Media PRO and More, it's a winning combination to create your own "Spotlight."

Phone: 877.605.6389

Website: anitamiranda.com

Email: transform@anitamiranda.com

LinkedIn: linkedIn.com/in/anitamiranda

Facebook: facebook.com/theanitamiranda

Twitter: @theanitamiranda

Ready to be a Published Author?

by Barb Anderson

10 DIY Tips: Niche, Memoirs or Storytelling

1. **As a business owner** – your unique experience and information should be shared with others; giving you credit as an expert in your field – published author has credibility, respect and a sense of accomplishment.

2. **Having a book** can help you grow your business in many ways and create more opportunities.

3. **Your book** can create a passive income.

4. **As a self-publisher**, you own all rights to your book, whereas a traditional publisher would likely own the rights. If they lose interest in your book, you cannot print additional copies unless you purchase those rights back.

5. **A traditional publisher** will finance the project, but may only offer a 5 – 20% royalty. Since most authors do their own promotion, why not self-publish and earn a 40 – 400% margin? If your book becomes a hit, publishers will come calling – this will give you the upper hand in negotiations.

6. **Control** - Self-publishing gives you the final say on the direction of your book. Your book reflects your vision and not someone else's.

7. **What are the Baby Boomers doing?** Most of them are approaching the end of their work cycle and are seeking new ways to monetize their services without having to be present. The promise of financial security from Social Security or corporate pensions is no longer viable. They are re-inventing themselves as speakers, trainers, coaches, and entrepreneurs with a multitude of experience to share.

8. **What can they do?** They can productize their knowledge and experience into profitable products.

9. **What are the Hot Items?** Books, CDs, DVDs, video training courses, audio products, webinars and enhanced eBooks are the rave.

10. **How do I offer these items?** Products can be sold from the back of the room after speaking or training. Most of these products can be sold from their website, from social media sites and available on demand.

11. **Bonus tip:** Do not forget Video Trailers.

Barb Anderson

Self-Publishing Strategist

As a Best-Selling Author and Award-Winning Publisher, Barb Anderson understands the importance and personal satisfaction of many Americans' dream of writing a book. If you've ever wanted to be a published author, it's easier than you think to fulfill that lifelong vision and also increase your market value. Your friends, prospects, and competitors will be amazed.

Besides the self-esteem boost (which is reason enough) and the dream accomplishment (even more reason), being a published author makes you a specialist. Depending on the industry or subject matter, it might even make you THE expert in your field. Which means that taking the time to write your book isn't just a foolish pursuit of a childhood dream; it's an important business and marketing strategy.

Let DM BookPro assist you in the process of creating your book.

Phone: 602.492.8932

Website: dmbookpro.com

Email: barb@dmbookpro.com

Facebook: facebook.com/dmbookpro

ANNE MCCOLL
COPYWRITER

Video Copywriting Tips

By Anne McColl

1. **Keep it short.** Statistics show that people will click away after two minutes. If you have a lot of information to cover, it might be more effective to make a series of videos, each addressing a specific subject or offering a tip.

2. **It's not about you.** Videos aren't home movies. Your video should offer information or answer a problem that a potential customer may have.

3. **Use plain English.** Despite what you may have learned in school, you don't get extra credit for using big words. Don't be bogged down in business jargon that doesn't mean anything.

4. **Tell your core message first.** State your big idea first, so if people click away, they haven't missed your primary message. After you communicate your main idea, then you can support it with stories and examples.

5. **Don't tell them. Show them.** This is video. Don't just talk about what a wonderful place your restaurant is. Show it in pictures.

6. **The less text the better.** Your screen shouldn't be filled with words. A few important words should convey your message and support your message.

7. **Always close with a call to action.** Always tell people what action you want them to take. It should tie back to a business goal – call this number. Download this white paper. Meet us at Booth 45.

8. **Make it personal.** People connect with people, not numbers. Your customers might not be moved statistics. Instead, tell a story about how you solved someone's problem or helped them achieve a goal. Then the numbers mean something.

9. **Don't get distracted by bells and whistles.** Just because you can use swirly sparkly transitions, doesn't mean you should. A good editor knows how to say no to elements that distract from the story.

10. **It's about them, not you.** It's easy to launch into a video and talk all about your business. Yawn. Instead, present your services as solutions to the problems and challenges your viewers face.

11. **Use music to add emotion.** Selecting the right piece of music can add an emotional punch to your message. Be careful that the music doesn't over power the rest of the audio on your video.

12. **The thumbnail counts.** Be sure the thumbnail of your video is graphically pleasing. It's like the cover of the a book and will greatly influence why someone clicks on your video or not.

13. **The title counts.** Just like a blog post, your video should have a catchy title. Sorry, if it's full of SEO keywords: yawn, yawn, yawn.

Anne McColl

I Help Brands Tell Stories

Anne McColl is a creative interactive copywriter. She helps brands and companies find the right words and pictures to tell their story. She's worked with some amazing brands, including Four Seasons Hotel, Hawaii Visitors Bureau, San Diego Zoo, WD-40, PETCO, Rubio's Fish Tacos, the Del Mar Fair, and with agencies of all sizes. Anne is a devoted design nerd and sits on the board of AIGA San Diego. When she's not surfing the Internet, she can often be found surfing the juicy waves of San Diego.

Phone: 619.261.4677

Website: annemccoll.com

LinkedIn: linkedin.com/in/annemccoll

Facebook: facebook.com/annemccoll

Twitter: @annemccoll

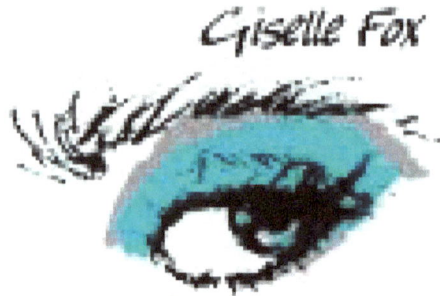

Make-Up Tips

By Giselle Fox

1. Concealers should always go on after foundation if using one and should be patted on with your ring finger and then blended out with a small fluffy or stipple brush.

2. Start in the inner corner of your eye and place small dots down to the middle of the eye or create a little triangle with the center point just below your iris. If your discoloration has a bluey cast, use a yellow based concealer as this cancels out the purple tones. Choose a peachy / rosier tone if your discoloration is much darker.

3. To cover blemishes or redness around the nose, use a more opaque concealer in a shade just a bit lighter than your foundation and with a more yellowish undertone, and apply with a very small brush, gently blending in the edges. Set the foundation and concealer with a powder. If things start looking cakey under your eyes throughout the day, add a tiny drop of moisturizer under your eye and gently blend it in and out until the cakey look dissolves.

4. Brightening eyes… A nude or white pencil drawn on the inner rims of your eyes will instantly make tired, red eyes look brighter. Also adding a bit in the inner corners drawn in a small triangle, will "open up" the eye.

5. When choosing eye shadow colors, always remember light colors "draw out" the eye and dark colors make the eye "recede."

6. If not using a Gel for eyebrows that helps your eyebrows stay in place, take a clean mascara wand and spray it with hairspray, then brush your eyebrows into place.

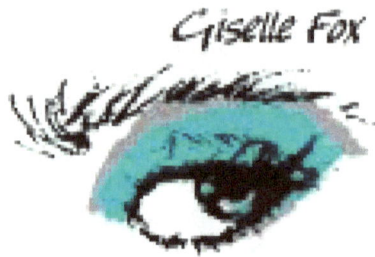

Beauty Kit Must Haves

By Giselle Fox

1. **Makeup Forever's** new **Ultra HD Invisible Makeup** and their **HD High Definition Finishing Powder**. Not only are these 2 products fabulous on camera but perfect for every day, too. The powder comes loose or in a compact and they make your skin look flawless.

2. A **Primer** is a must too, as it makes foundation look so much smoother.

3. Some of my very favorite **brushes** that clients always comment on when I use them are **Real Techniques by Samantha Chapman**. Their brush designed for Blusher is actually what I use for powders. Perfect size and it delivers the powders beautifully. Their setting brush is also a favorite for lightly blending in concealers so they look seamless and it's great for touch ups on the face for powders. **ELF Cosmetics** makes a black handle stipple brush also, which I use to blend in foundations. Very inexpensive!! All of these brushes rival the more expensive brands and clean really easily.

4. I also love **MAC's Mineralize Powders**, which are lightweight and give a medium coverage without looking cakey.

5. I am really enjoying these new **Gel Eye Pencils** that many companies are now making. So much easier to use on yourself than the potted gels. They are almost all waterproof and stay on for hours without smudging.

6. Lastly, **Clean n Clear** has fabulous **blotting tissues** that leave no residue on the skin and really pick up the oil so you don't have to keep adding powder.

Giselle Fox

Welcome to Makeup Artistry

A professional makeup and hair artist for over 30 years, Giselle's extensive experience includes television, print, live events, corporate CBT and video. A former model and actress, Giselle understands the meaning of "camera ready" and is an integral member of the production team.

Her clients are local, national, and international with the mediums being film, Hi Def, video, and print.

Giselle is an expert in beautiful "lifestyle" looks, and also specializes in fashion/beauty, stylized and some special effects.

Phone: 480.688.9874

Website: gisellefox.shutterfly.com

Email: gisellefox_makeup@hotmail.com

Skyler McCurine

Redefining the Look of Leadership

Skyler McCurine is redefining the standard of beauty in America as a personal stylist, public speaker, wonder woman and founder of Le Red Balloon. Driven by the lackluster stereotypical portrayal of women in the media, she leads workshops for teenage girls and professional women around conscious media consumption, leadership, self-acceptance, personal branding, and of course, style. Skyler reminds her clients that they are beautiful, just as they are, not after 20 pounds or after a new wardrobe, but just as they are, today. When Skyler is not busy trying to change the world, she is brazenly venturing through it, getting lost in the beauty, and leaving a trail of red balloons behind her. She enjoys jazz, decoupaging, laughter, bare feet and occasionally indulges in copious amounts of champagne.

Phone: 619.512.3744

Website: leredballoon.com

LinkedIn: linkedin.com/in/skylermccurine

Facebook: facebook.com/leredballoon

Twitter: @leredballoon

Video Equipment Recommendations

Using a Smartphone as a Camera

If you are using a smartphone as a camera, you'll want a simple, but effective tripod like the following.

PEMOTech® Mini Tripod Universal Octopus Style Mount

A simple, but effective tabletop tripod for all Apple and Android phones.

http://tiny.cc/brgk7x

ChargerCity MegaGrab2 Easy-Adjust Smartphone Holder Mount & 360° Swivel Adjustment Selfie Video Recording Camera Tripod Adapter

This adapter is for those who already have a tripod or are getting a regular one, but want to be able to use it for their phone. It works for both the Iphone and for most Android phones.

http://tiny.cc/evgk7x

191

Cameras

One of the most important pieces of equipment is your camera. If you would like something of a higher caliber than your smartphone, here are some options:

Kodak PlayTouch Video Camera

This camera records in 1080p HD and is compatible with 32 GB SD cards. It allows you to see more details and accurate colors in low light. It has an external microphone jack that lets you record in stereo.

http://tiny.cc/a5gk7x

Canon EOS Rebel T3i Digital Camera SLR Kit

A full kit with a wonderful, quality video camera. It includes lenses, a 16 GB SD card, flash, a carrying case, and more.

http://tiny.cc/i8gk7x

Tripods

A good tripod can be just as important as a good camera.

Ravelli APLT2 50" Light Weight Aluminum Tripod with Bag

A good, solid tripod that extends to a height of 49 inches.

http://tiny.cc/0dhk7x

Lighting

A set's lighting has a strong effect on the final look of the shot, so you want to be sure to have a great lighting set-up.

Fancierstudio 3000 Watt Digital Video Continuous Softbox Lighting Kit

A nice quality lighting kit perfect for a 3-point lighting set-up. The lights come with softboxes, a great addition for video.

http://tiny.cc/nghk7x

Microphones

You want to have audio that sounds nice and clear, so you will want an external microphone.

ATian SGC-698 Photography Interview MIC Microphone

A nice, consumer quality mic that will pick up audio better than your camera's internal mic.

http://tiny.cc/hkhk7x

Audio-Technica ATR-3350 Lavalier Omnidirectional Condenser Microphone

A good quality omni-directional lavalier. It is mono, not stereo, so keep that in mind.

http://tiny.cc/jthk7x

SD Cards

When using a digital camera, you'll need an sd card with a a fair amount of space, as you'll need it to record video.

Transcend 32 GB Class 10 SDHC Flash Memory Card

A quick and efficient SD card with palnty of space for all of your video needs. As a class 10 card, it will easily be able to capture your video with no problems. It is usable with any camera that can use a class 10 SD card.

http://tiny.cc/z1hk7x

Editing Programs

There are plenty of quality video editing programs out there. If you only plan on creating the occasional video, programs such as Movie Maker and IMovie will work just fine. However, if you plan on creating a lot of high-quality videos, it would be wise to look into a program like Adobe Premier or Final Cut Pro.

Red Carpet Academy Workshop
Photo Gallery

Before

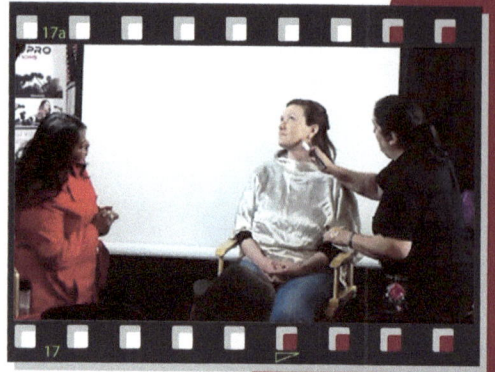

197

RedCarpetAcademy.org

After

201

Vocabulary

Audio Check - A test of the volume of your voice; you'll typically be asked to count to ten by an audio engineer.

B-roll - Video footage that shows action without sound.

Bust Shot - Chest-to-Head shot framed above the elbows.

Chroma Key - The process of putting a virtual background into a video during post-production. Used in tandem with green screen.

Close-up (CU) - A close view of an actor or an object, featuring details isolated from their surroundings. A close-up of an actor typically shows only his head.

Cue - A signal (as a word, phrase, or bit of stage business) to a performer to begin a specific speech or action

Cue Card - A card held beside a camera for a television broadcaster to read from while appearing as if looking into the camera.

Elevator Pitch – A brief and effective sales speech.

EPK - Electronic Press Kit. Includes video and stills to promote a product or service.

Establishing Shot - A camera shot, usually at long range, that identifies or establishes the location of a scene.

Extreme Close-up (XCU) - A very close view of an actor or an object featuring minute details. An extreme close-up of an actor typically shows only his eyes or part of his face.

Extreme Long Shot (XLS) - A panoramic view of a film scene, photographed from a great distance

Eyeline - Where a subject appears to be looking, typically into the camera or screen left/right.

Frame – Look for horizontal and vertical lines in the frame (e.g. the horizon, poles, etc). Make sure the horizontals are level, and the verticals are straight up and down.

Full Shot - A long shot that includes the human body in full within the frame

Green Screen - The backdrop against which an interview or action is filmed that allows a computerized or virtual background to be inserted during post-production.

Headroom, Looking Room, & Leading Room - These terms refer to the amount of room in the frame which is strategically left empty.

Head Shot - Just a talking head. Rarely used in live TV because people move too much.

Jump Cut - An abrupt transition from one scene or clip to another.

Lavaliere Mic - A small microphone that clips to your shirt or jacket. Often called a lav.

Live Streaming - Live video content delivered over the Internet.

Live Shot - A live broadcast of a reporter speaking to the camera, typically done from the field.

Long Shot (LS) - A shot that shows a fairly broad view of a subject within its setting. A long shot of an actor typically includes his entire body and much of his surroundings.

Mark - Your spot for the scene will be marked on the floor, usually in a n X or T formation with some glaring piece of colored tape.

Medium Shot (MS) - A relatively close shot that shows part of a person or object in some detail. A medium shot of an actor typically shows his body from the knees or waist up

Package - A video story edited together that typically includes interview soundbites, b-roll footage, a recorded voice over (track), and a stand-up from a reporter; usually between one to three minutes long.

Rule of Thirds - This rule divides the frame into nine sections, as in the first frame below. Points (or lines) of interest should occur at 1/3 or 2/3 of the way up (or across) the frame, rather than in the center.

Selfie – A picture one takes of one's self, usually with a smartphone or tablet.

Sit-down Interview - A recorded interview that a reporter may edit for soundbites or broadcast in its entirety.

Soundbite - An edited clip of a recorded interview, typically 8-30 seconds long.

"Standby on the Set" - This means "attention" and "quiet"on the set. The command is given 15-30 seconds before rolling tape.

Stand-up - a video clip of a reporter talking directly to the camera, from the field. Also called piece-to-camera.

Teleprompter - A machine that displays text directly under the camera lens to prompt the person speaking; also called an autocue.

Track - A narrator or reporter's voice recorded on tape and edited together with b-roll; "to track" is to read and record your script. Also called VO or voice over.

Two-shot - A medium shot featuring two actors

Wide Shot - Normally the full setting, stage edge-to-stage edge, top to bottom within a frame.

~About The Author~

Lights! Camera! Action! Anita never imagined that one day she would be a Director, Videographer, Advocate & Author... now she's living her dream! It wasn't always that way. It would have been easy to let insecurity, hard knocks, and past life experiences defeat her. Growing up as a ward of the court, Anita was terrified of being photographed. Instead of letting the fear control and define her, she faced her fear head-on. This move became Miranda's KISS, Keep Image Simply Successful. Anita took her studies one step beyond, examining the ins and outs of videography and photography. She learned the techniques of how celebrities are taught to present themselves to the camera, as well as utilizing camera angles, natural and studio lighting, hair and makeup artistry, camera-ready wardrobe selection, and studio and on location staging. Through her journey of self-doubt, not thinking she was "thin" enough, and other excuses women and men commonly tell themselves, Anita developed her own confidence and turned her talents to helping others, beginning with the **Red Carpet Academy DIY Media Kit**. Anita made a choice to earn a Master's degree and be the creator of her own destiny!

Anita's passion for helping those less fortunate inspired her to establish Circle of Helping Hands (COHH) a 501(c)(3). With COHH, Media PRO and More, and her recent endeavor, Living Disabled NOT Dead, Anita has one mission: help others reclaim their power and recognize what is brilliant, special and unique about themselves. Her team is successful in helping navigate and maneuver the red tape around the system to secure their rightful benefits, find employment, and offer solutions. Currently she assists Veterans, Women, and their Children, so that they too may leave behind a legacy of hope and promise for people who follow in their footsteps.

RedCarpetAcademy.org

~About The Co-Author~

In her teen years, Samantha enjoyed nearly every kind of art. Introduced to video editing in high school, she expanded her creativity and discovered a new form of art. Soon, she was creating, editing, and producing her very own videos. She enjoyed the delicacy of all the components and how they intertwined. Her attention to details, critical thinking, and can-do attitude allowed Samantha to express herself and others.

She researched her options and made the choice to move by herself, her first time away from home, to pursue her dreams. She chose Collins College due to the extensive curriculum offered through their programs. In her first semester she was and continued to be on the Dean's Honor Roll. Her other passion is writing, and she graduated as a member of the Collins Creative Writing Club. She is also working on her first novel, Oz: A New Beginning.

Samantha Leiter has earned an AA in Digital Video Production (2010) and a BA in Film and Video Production (2012), both from Collins College. She has interned at Miranda's Creatives, LLC since June 2011 and quickly advanced to senior editor in-training, senior special effects in-training, and is their resident expert with Photoshop. There, she has worked with editing, compositing, graphics, photography, motion graphics, and production. She has created speaker demos, highlight videos, and videos for businesses. She is also the FX expert for Media PRO and More, allowing her to work extensively with virtual sets/green screen.

Samantha does editing, illustrating, and proofreading for Beacon Publishing House and Living Disabled Publishing.

Other Books By Anita Miranda

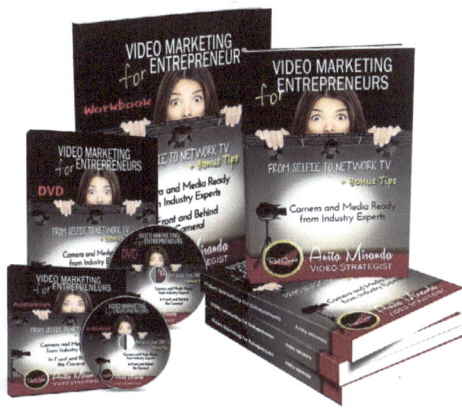

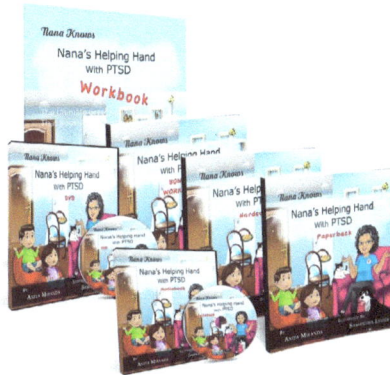

Scan Me

http://tiny.cc/nsd2yx
to get your copy

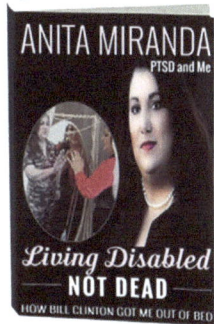

Beacon
Publishing House

Nana Knows PTSD: Paperback, Hardcover, Workbook,
DVD, Audio & Other Publications Available.
Other Titles Coming Soon.

RedCarpetAcademy.org

www.ingramcontent.com/pod-product-compliance
Lightning Source LLC
Chambersburg PA
CBHW050839220326
41598CB00006B/406